Rebecca Sitton's Spelling Sourcebook™ 1

Your Guide for Developing Research-Based Spelling Instruction for the Writing-Rich Classroom

ISBN 1-886050-00-7

Egger Publishing, Inc.
P.O. Box 12248, Scottsdale, AZ 85267
Phone: 888-WE-SPELL (888-937-7355)
FAX: 480-951-2276

15 14 13 12 11 10 9 8 7 6

Rebecca Sitton's

SPELLING SOURCEBOOK™ SERIES

SOURCEBOOKS

- "How-To" and "Why"
  Your source for developing research-based spelling instruction for the writing-rich classroom.
  Sourcebook 1 Necessary for teachers in all grades.
- Activities
  Your source for skill-based activities for teaching and extending the high-use writing words.
  Sourcebook 2 Words 1–400 (grades 1–4)
  Sourcebook 3 Words 401–800 (grades 5–6)
  Sourcebook 4 Words 801–1200 (grades 7-8)
- Assessment
  Your source for blackline master Cloze Activities and Dictation Sentences for the high-use writing words.
  Sourcebook Reviews Words 1–400 (grades 1–4) accompanies *Sourcebook 2*
  Sourcebook Reviews Words 401–800 (grades 5–6) accompanies *Sourcebook 3*
  Sourcebook Reviews Words 801–1200 (grades 7–8) accompanies *Sourcebook 4*
- Word-Wise Sourcebooks
  Your source for laugh-aloud rhymes for learning language skills.
  Level 1 *Wordy Birdy* (grades 1–2)
  Level 2 *Willy Wordster* (grades 3–4)
  Level 3 *Inspector Clue-So* (grades 5–6)

VIDEOS

- **Staff Development Video Series**
  Tape I Introduction to Teachers (85 min.)
  Tape II Grading and Management (92 min.)
  Tape III Introduction to Parents (37 min.)
  Video Training Guide
- **Free Preview Video**
  On-loan overview
  Call Egger Publishing, Inc.
  toll free: 888-937-7355 *(888-WE-SPELL)*

SEMINAR HANDBOOK

- **Increasing Student Spelling Achievement**

CLASSROOM AIDS

- **My Spell Check K–2**
  Your students' source for an alphabetical listing of 85 high-use writing words with colorful references for animals, numbers, family, clothes, school, days, months, food, and weather. Each package includes a teacher resource of over 50 word activities to extend the word bank, and ten 8 1/2" x 11" coated student cards.
- **Spell Check 3–8**
  Your students' source for an alphabetical listing of 150 high-use writing words with references for months, days, common abbreviations, and 75 context sentences for often-confused words. Each package includes a teacher resource of over 50 word activities to extend the word bank, and ten 8 1/2" x 11" coated student cards.
- **Wall Charts**
  Your source for 5 colorful classroom charts:
  - Alphabetical list of the 100 high-use writing words
  - Context sentences for the "there" homophones
  - Context sentences for the "to" homophones
  - Prefix poem
  - Independent word-study procedure.

  Each package contains all five 18" x 24" wall charts.

TO ORDER

Northwest Textbook
800-676-6630

QUESTIONS

- Call toll free: 888-937-7355 *(888-WE-SPELL)*
- Write to us: Egger Publishing, Inc.
  P.O. Box 12248
  Scottsdale, AZ 85267
- Find us: www.sittonspelling.com
- e-mail Rebecca: rsitton@sittonspelling.com

Dear Educator,

I have created the ***Spelling Sourcebook*** Series for you as an alternative to traditional workbook spelling. It is your source for teacher-customized spelling instruction designed to complement the writing-rich classroom and form the foundation for systematic instruction of basic spelling skills. You can develop your own research-based, spelling-for-writing program using the ***Spelling Sourcebook*** options and resources.

Begin with this book, ***Spelling Sourcebook 1.*** This specific guidebook tells you how to develop and implement your own spelling program using high-frequency writing words. The seventeen Articles of Part 1 include options for dividing the high-use words across the grades, organizing a flexible schedule for teaching the words, and establishing practical expectations for spelling accountability in writing; guidelines for effectively using research-based procedures, informing parents and involving them in the new program, and handling lower and higher achievers; and suggestions for authentic and performance-based spelling evaluations. Part 2 of ***Spelling Sourcebook 1*** is the reference section. It features 1200 high-frequency writing words listed in their order of frequency of use, practical spelling rules, game and writing ideas, and a review of valid spelling research with a complete bibliography. The final section, Part 3, has your blackline master forms for instruction and record keeping.

Spelling Sourcebooks 2, 3, and ***4*** are your activity books that offer a menu of options for ensuring the development of basic spelling skills. They provide abundant suggestions for teaching and extending the high-use words within a literature-based, language-centered classroom. ***Spelling Sourcebook 2*** includes ideas for words within the frequencies 1–400. ***Spelling Sourcebooks 3*** and ***4*** follow with ideas for words 401–800 and 801–1200. The three ***Spelling Sourcebook Reviews*** for high-use writing words complement ***Spelling Sourcebooks 2, 3,*** and ***4.*** The ***Reviews*** are your source for Blackline Master Cloze Activities and Dictation Sentences for every set of five sequential high-use writing words 1–1200. They provide systematic reinforcement of previously introduced words for ongoing practice and evaluation toward the mastery of the words in writing. Then, the three ***Word-Wise Sourcebooks*** provide laugh-aloud rhymes for entertaining extension of multiple language and spelling skills.

There are no student books, only teacher resource books. You don't need student exercise books with the ***Spelling Sourcebook*** Series. Spelling practice takes place every day in writing across the curriculum, complemented by your systematic selection of ready-to-go activities for developing students' basic spelling and language skills. Using the guidelines in the various teacher ***Sourcebooks,*** your spelling program will provide more practice than the fill-in-the-blanks exercise books were ever able to offer you!

I invite you to participate in the ***Spelling Sourcebook*** methodology. This nontraditional, commonsense approach to spelling will help your students learn to spell where it counts . . . in their everyday writing!

If you have questions, contact me. If you'd like to share your experiences using the ***Spelling Sourcebook*** Series, contact me. Or if you'd like information on the spelling seminar I present to educators that highlights the concepts of the ***Spelling Sourcebook*** methodology, contact me. I'd like to hear from you.

Sincerely,

Rebecca Sitton

Rebecca Sitton
P.O. Box 12248
Scottsdale, AZ 85267
888-WE-SPELL
E-mail: rsitton@sittonspelling.com

Your Guide to the Contents

Defining the Spelling Curriculum

Why is spelling important?

Spelling is a skill. It is a basic communication skill. And it *is* important. Regardless of how well writers express their ideas in writing, if their writing in its final form has misspellings, the worth of the message is diminished in the eyes of the reader. In fact, the personal worth of the writer may also be diminished.

Ask employers if misspellings on job applications and resumes influence their opinion of applicants. Ask yourself how your own opinion of a person you've never met might be affected if his or her letter to you contains misspellings. Spelling errors convey a subtle message of limited knowledge or a lack of conscientious effort on the part of the writer.

Acceptance, then, is one reason for teaching spelling. Writing that conforms to conventional English orthography is more acceptable to the reader. But there is another reason for teaching spelling. Writers who have a mental bank of words that they can spell correctly with ease while writing have a fluidity to their writing that poor spellers do not have.

All teachers have observed students who "turn off" to writing because they lack a mental bank of spelling words from which to draw as they write. These students learn that the less they write, the less they misspell. They lack a ready resource for spelling the words they need as they write. Spelling instruction helps students develop a mental bank of high-use words. Then, as they write, they can focus their attention on the content of the message being written, rather than on the mechanics of writing it.

Why will technology never make spelling instruction obsolete?

Yet, these reasons do not convince some people that spelling is an essential skill. They point out that dictionaries are affordable and easily available. Further, technology is capable of providing spelling aid through spell-checkers and grammar-checkers on word processors. Shouldn't writers be taught to use these spelling resources? Yes—but they're not enough.

The teaching of computation was not forsaken when calculators became a household item. However, neither a calculator nor a spell-checker can think . . . and there is no substitute for thinking. A spell-checker does not alert the writer to an incorrectly spelled word when the spelling would be correct for another word. For instance, the errors in this sentence do not register on a spell-checker, nor do all the errors register on a grammar-checker:

Their our for pairs. (There are four pears.)

Advocates for abandoning the spelling curriculum go on to cite research that clearly indicates that spelling is developmental. They say that if educators would familiarize themselves with the natural, predictable steps through which children progress as they acquire spelling skills, a spelling program would no longer make good sense.

How do developmental skills develop?

Yes, spelling is developmental. Much research reports the developmental nature of spelling. These reports are highly interesting and factual reading. But isn't the acquisition of all skills developmental? Why single out spelling as being unique? Children learn to count before they are taught to add . . . they learn to add before they are taught to multiply—learning number concepts is developmental. And does it logically follow that if something is developmental, it cannot or should not be taught? Do all developmental skills develop completely naturally, making a curriculum for their mastery unnecessary?

Why is a curriculum necessary?

The first obligation of conscientious educators is to be knowledgeable of how students develop and learn. Then, however, they must apply this knowledge to implement instructional strategies to enhance student learning. A stated curriculum provides the foundation for this instruction and suggests strategies for achieving, or developing, the desired learning. And it is irresponsible to assume that all teachers can intuitively create such a curriculum while juggling the demands of everyday instruction.

So, yes, the ***Spelling Sourcebooks*** *do* call for a stated spelling curriculum, albeit a significant departure from traditional spelling methodology. Indeed, the scope and sequence of the ***Spelling Sourcebook*** curriculum is sensitive to the developmental steps of spelling acquisition, but provides teachers with options for contributing to spelling growth as their students develop as writers. Just knowing the developmental stages of spelling growth does not provide teachers with a plan for what to do Monday with a classroom full of students.

*What is traditional about the **Sourcebook** curriculum? What is nontraditional?*

The ***Spelling Sourcebook*** curriculum is the spelling complement to a literature-based, writing-rich classroom steeped in language experiences. Traditional, commonsense spelling skills and their application in writing are built into the methodology through systematic instruction. Teachers are empowered through the ***Spelling Sourcebooks*** to make many curriculum decisions that the traditional spelling books once made for them. These decisions that customize spelling instruction to accommodate a variety of needs are made from a menu of carefully researched options, all of which are bonded to basic skill development, writing, and research.

Therefore, the ***Spelling Sourcebook*** curriculum is considerably more flexible, less structured than that of the traditional spelling series. It may be that some teachers will initially feel uncomfortable with the freedom this flexibility provides. Nonetheless, sufficient structure is provided so that spelling instruction is *not* incidental. Spelling instruction using the ***Spelling Sourcebook*** methodology follows a clear and logical plan.

How do current spelling instructional outcomes measure up to employers' expectations for workplace literacy?

Basic literacy, specifically spelling competence, must be one of education's ensured outcomes. Employers are not asking too much of educators when they plead for graduates to be equipped with basic language know-how skills to function literately in the workplace. Spelling high-use words consistently correctly is a component of this literacy.

Unfortunately, facts clearly indicate that many students are not currently learning to spell these high-use words correctly in their everyday writing. A look at their writing verifies this. Often even the most capable students misspell commonly-used words in their writing.

Why is the Friday Test an invalid assessment?

Yes, these students spell the words correctly on a spelling test! But spelling on a spelling test is not an authentic assessment of spelling facility. Employers do not give spelling tests on Friday to determine whether their employees are literate written communicators. Nonetheless, some teachers may believe they have successfully taught spelling when their students score well on a dictated list of words written correctly on demand in isolation, apart from writing. This test is the traditional weekly "Friday Spelling Test."

Ironically, the words on these tests are often the difficult, seldom-used words. Spelling instruction, then, frequently encourages memorizing letter sequences of words that have little pertinence for everyday writing . . . week after week for the Friday Test.

Traditionally, the grades on these tests, rather than the presence or absence of misspelled words in the students' writing, become the measure of students' spelling ability. It is not unusual for students to receive top spelling grades, yet show a serious lack of attention to spelling in their writing. What message does this give the student writer?

Why aren't students transferring spelling skills into writing?

Are students incapable of learning to spell words correctly in their everyday writing? No, of course students can learn to spell in their writing! Then why haven't they learned? The answer is an obvious one. Students are not spelling words responsibly in their everyday writing because they don't have to.

Most educators simply don't expect students to spell correctly in their everyday writing. "Oh, I *do* expect my students to spell!" object some teachers. They adamantly believe that they maintain high standards for spelling in writing because they firmly tell their students to proofread their papers. Yet, students know that their spelling grades are based on spelling words correctly on a test, not on spelling in everyday assignments across the curriculum. Again, what message does this give the student writer? Or . . . what message does it give the student writer if *no* grades are given for spelling?

In fact, be forewarned . . . inattention to spelling literacy jeopardizes the language-centered approach to learning, as well as the credibility of teachers and schools. Students must be expected to spell an increasing number of high-use words correctly in their writing as they mature as writers. This does not inhibit their creativity. It is basic literacy. In fact, if students learn that it's acceptable to spell irresponsibly throughout their schooling, serious problems may develop when they later find that employers have higher expectations for them than their teachers had. Worst case, their job applications are not considered because of inexcusable spelling errors.

How does a traditional definition of spelling mastery differ from the new one?

Spelling is not how many words a teacher "covers," nor how many words a student spells correctly on a spelling test, albeit a Friday Test or a standardized spelling test. Covering words and then testing students on them reflect an inaccurate concept of spelling mastery. Spelling mastery is the ability to spell words correctly in everyday writing.

Can schools accommodate this definition of spelling mastery? Yes, but "spelling for writing" will not evolve through traditional spelling instructional methods and assessment tools. The old-time spelling textbooks and the philosophy on which they were founded must *go.*

"No spelling book? Then what will teachers do for spelling?" The spelling book is . . . well, traditional. Yet, most educators concede that the traditional spelling program has failed. If spelling mastery means spelling well in everyday writing, then the spelling textbooks have not satisfactorily met the challenge. Nonetheless, the books are difficult to do without . . . they have conveniently filled a time frame that provides seatwork practice within a subject area that teachers are expected to teach . . . and that parents expect their children to learn.

What role has the traditional spelling textbook served?

Contrary to time-honored tradition, spelling can successfully be taught without the aid of the customary student spelling textbooks. In fact, in some instances these spelling textbooks may have hindered the acquisition of spelling skills in writing. Why? Because the spelling books became the spelling curriculum. There were 36 weekly units of words, and conscientious teachers felt an admirable obligation to teach and test every one of them. And *that* was spelling.

Instruction in the spelling books did not consider the needs of the student writers. It did not encourage students to spell and proofread outside of the spelling book. Spelling became an isolated subject, apart from purposeful writing, void of pertinence and utility.

However, there is no guarantee that removing the spelling textbooks from classrooms will result in better spelling instruction. Teachers in classrooms without spelling textbooks have clearly shown this to be true. Unless the old spelling programs are replaced with practical, more effective ways of teaching spelling that produce visible spelling proficiencies in writing, the problem remains unsolved. The solution requires that spelling find a meaningful role within the integrated curriculum. This necessitates a change in conventional thinking about what spelling mastery is and when it has been achieved. This change may not be easy, but it will be exciting and the results will be gratifying . . . and the change is overdue.

What alternative is there to "textbook" spelling?

The ***Spelling Sourcebook*** Series provides the guidelines for this change. The methodology, as suggested through the ***Spelling Sourcebooks***, is a departure from the "tired and traditional" spelling textbook programs. The ***Spelling Sourcebook*** Series shows forward-looking educators how to develop and use a spelling program of their own . . . one *without* student textbooks. Yet, students get far more spelling practice than ever before. Students practice spelling every time they write. This everyday practice is complemented by systematic instruction in basic skills that are teacher-selected from an extensive menu of ready-to-go lessons. No longer are teachers married to the canned lessons in the student practice books that purported to be appropriate for every child on a given day. No longer is assessment a game of memorizing word lists for the Friday Test, but instead parallels real-life use of spelling within the context of writing. So, the ***Spelling Sourcebook*** Series provides a befitting and timely alternative to yesterday's spelling curriculum.

How will changes in the spelling curriculum emerge?

Implementation of the ideas in the ***Spelling Sourcebooks*** requires leadership. The leaders must have the courage to stand up to the status quo and the tenacity to struggle with the limitations of the educational resources needed for this change. They must be committed to reshaping the thinking surrounding spelling instruction. Then, they must be on-the-spot with ***Spelling Sourcebook*** suggestions for instruction and assessment to replace the old ways.

This new leadership role is not for everyone. It is certainly not for those educators incapable of seeing the future; it is not for those who have a hundred reasons why students can't or shouldn't be expected to spell; it is not for those who avoid the issue by promising that spelling skills will develop naturally . . . *later;* it is not for the nay sayers and complainers undaunted by cries for school reform. It is, however, for those who have a passion for educational excellence and a sense of purpose dedicated to equipping all students with language literacy. Educators open to this challenge, read on.

Customizing the Program: How to Get Started

What is the first step in creating a spelling program?

Once educators recognize the problems plaguing current spelling practices and are committed to their solution, an initial priority is creating the instructional tool to aid the change. The ***Spelling Sourcebooks*** provide the foundation and guidelines for customizing a program tailored to the needs of specific teachers and students. Perhaps the first step is shaping a spelling Core Curriculum from which all the teaching and learning can emerge. Basic to the spelling Core Curriculum is the choice of spelling words.

Why is it irresponsible to have students choose all their own spelling words?

Some expert educators are convinced that students should choose all their own spelling words based on their personal reading and writing experiences. They say, "Children are capable of selecting the words they need, want, and are ready for, and should learn them through a variety of spelling strategies and resources that totally immerse the child in writing." Given this principle, exactly how does a school district, school, or individual teacher provide for the implementation, management, and assessment of such an unstructured program?

A strong curriculum does not just happen. It is shaped through a conscientious formulation of specific goals and objectives that support the desired learning outcomes. These outcomes must be clearly defined, with the options and tools to achieve them specifically stated. Because spelling is not an incidental skill, an effective spelling curriculum cannot emerge from an open-ended philosophy based on what individual children deem appropriate for themselves to learn at any given time.

Yet, within an effective spelling curriculum, it is essential to provide opportunities for individual students and teachers to generate some of their own spelling words based on current needs and interests. These words and other additional words *complement* the Core Curriculum. But without a Core Curriculum, the complement becomes a boat without a sail.

What is the main source of words for a spelling program correlated to writing?

Selecting the words for the Core Curriculum, or Core Words, poses little challenge for educators whose philosophy is founded on the premise that spelling must be pertinent to everyday writing. This philosophical base dictates that the Core Words must be high-frequency words used throughout a lifetime of everyday writing. Several massive studies have been done over the years that tabulate word frequencies in writing. Conscientious spelling instruction must use this research for compiling the spelling Core Word list.

Spelling Sourcebook 1 provides a cross-referenced compilation of these high-frequency writing words (see Reference 1, page 77). There are 1200 high-utility writing words in the ***Spelling Sourcebook*** word bank. These 1200 words provide the source for customizing a list of Core Words for a specific group of students and teachers using the ***Spelling Sourcebook*** methodology.

The words in the word bank are listed in the order of their frequency of use in everyday writing. The lower the number of the word in the word bank, the higher its long-term utility is in everyday writing. The total list of 1200 words conservatively represents over 90% of the words used in adult and student writing.

How can the choice of spelling words affect spelling literacy in writing?

Following are the number of words that constitute the percentages of use of the Core Words in adult writing:

first 8 words	18% of all words used in writing
first 25 words	33% of all words used in writing
first 100 words	50% of all words used in writing
first 1,000 words	89% of all words used in writing

The percentages for student writers are higher than the percentages indicated here. Student writers use fewer words, so the repetitions of these words are greater. This results in higher percentages. For example, the first 100 words is approximately 68% of the total words used in student writing.

What implications do these percentages have for effective spelling instruction? Surely, developing writers can learn to spell and proofread the first 100 high-use words. The sooner these words are mastered, the sooner a student's writing provides visible evidence that spelling has been taught. And, in a nutshell, that is *why* spelling is being taught . . . for writing! The results of spelling instruction must be clearly visible in everyday writing.

Which words should be introduced first?

For the tightest bond between spelling instruction and everyday writing, the Core Words should be introduced in the order of their frequency of use. Words with the highest utility in everyday writing need to be introduced before words with lower writing utility. Beginning writers, then, need to be introduced to the most powerful words in writing. These high-use words provide an instant spelling proficiency regardless of the writing topic. And this early success further develops student motivation to write.

To ensure an orderly instructional progression through the Core Words by all teachers, the words should be divided consecutively by grade level. The grade-level divisions customize the ***Spelling Sourcebook*** word bank to meet the needs of specific teachers and students.

How can the Core Words be divided by grade level?

To develop grade-level lists of Core Words using the word bank, a decision must be made as to how many words each grade level wishes to assume the responsibility for introducing. This progression through the words can begin when student writers have acquired the skills to comfortably read the words at the beginning of the word bank. This is usually the second half of first grade (see Article 16, page 67). The progression ends with the last grade level that is implementing the ***Spelling Sourcebook*** methodology. Generally, teachers should assign a limited number of words to first grade and have no more than two hundred words per grade at the upper levels.

How can the Core Words be divided by grade levels?

Following are two examples of the many different ways the words could be divided consecutively among grade levels to customize the program to meet various needs.

Example 1:

grade 1	word frequencies 1–30	(30 words)
grade 2	word frequencies 31–130	(100 words)
grade 3	word frequencies 131–265	(135 words)
grade 4	word frequencies 266–400	(135 words)
grade 5	word frequencies 401–600	(200 words)
grade 6	word frequencies 601–800	(200 words)
grade 7	word frequencies 801–1000	(200 words)
grade 8	word frequencies 1001–1200	(200 words)

A spelling program that encompasses only grades 1–6 does not need to accommodate all 1200 words within grades 1–6. It is always better to teach fewer words well than to teach many words poorly. Effective spelling instruction is not "covering" long lists of words.

Example 2 reflects Core Words drawn from a smaller word bank—just the first 800 of the 1200 total words in the word bank.

Example 2:

grade 1	word frequencies 1–25	(25 words)
grade 2	word frequencies 26–115	(90 words)
grade 3	word frequencies 116–250	(135 words)
grade 4	word frequencies 251–400	(150 words)
grade 5	word frequencies 401–600	(200 words)
grade 6	word frequencies 601–800	(200 words)

Once the number of Core Words has been determined and divided by grade level using the ***Spelling Sourcebook*** word bank as the resource, teachers can be presented with their new Core Word Curriculum. The Core Words are a customized set of words divided by grade level to accommodate a specific group of program users. The grade-level divisions for the customized set of Core Words should be recorded here as a resource for teachers using the program:

How has my school or school district divided the Core Words for teachers?

The Core Words by Grade Level

grades	word frequencies	number of words

Are the Core Words the total program?

The Core Words divided by grade levels are not the "program," they are the seeds from which the program grows, or develops. They provide a foundation for each grade level to begin growing spelling and related skills and concepts and a springboard for the addition of hundreds of words for further exposure and discussion. The major assessment for the program is not a test of these Core Words, but a routine and random checking of a subset of the Core Words, called Priority Words (see Article 8, page 33, and Article 9, page 39), that students are always expected to spell correctly in their everyday writing.

How do the Core Words differ in function from traditional word lists?

The Core Words cannot be likened to the word lists in a traditional program. In a traditional program, the word lists tried unsuccessfully to serve two purposes. First, they were the foundation for spelling skill development. The words in each unit illustrated a specific skill, such as a phonic pattern. This worked well for teaching skills, yet this method occasionally forced the inclusion of words into the word lists with little writing relevance. Second, these words were also the "spelling words" to be learned. Yet, experience confirms that these words were not learned long term, but learned only for a Friday Test. After the test, the students were not graded on these words again, with the exception of their possible inclusion in the Six Week Review test. There was no accountability for these words in writing. Therefore, the traditional programs achieved skill development through their word lists, but failed to achieve spelling accountability for these words.

In the ***Sourcebook*** methodology, both skill development and accountability are achieved. The Core Words, like the traditional word lists, are the foundation for skill development. All the traditional skills are developed. The ***Sourcebook*** approach further relates these skills to language learning across the curriculum to create fully integrated learning. Then a subset of the Core Words, the Priority Words, are identified for accountability in writing. This occurs after the students have had multiple activities with these words over time through the ***Sourcebook*** activity options. So, skill growth and spelling accountability in writing are wholly achieved through the ***Sourcebook*** approach to spelling literacy. This is achieved through a set of words for skill development and another set of words for accountability. Albeit, each of these sets of words are high-use writing words that create a bond between spelling and writing.

How do students learn to spell the Core Words?

Although the Core Words are those words designated as the words for skill development, students do indeed learn them through repeated exposure to them. Unlike the traditional word-list words that disappeared after the Friday Test, the Core Words in the ***Sourcebook*** methodology are revisited again and again through subsequent activities for ongoing practice. This repetition far exceeds the limited exposure students received for their spelling words in the old practice books. Now students are afforded continuous practice that provides them the opportunity to learn the words permanently.

On what days should spelling units begin and end?

Each Core Word unit need not have the same number of Core Words, be taught within a weekly Monday-through-Friday time frame, nor have the same number of support activities. It is important to remember that students are practicing spelling every time they write through their accountability for their Priority Words. This provides more spelling practice than ever before! The Core Word activities complement this ongoing spelling-in-context practice with skill development activities. This skill development should be routinely included in the program within a comfortable time frame for teaching.

How are the activities chosen for each unit?

Teachers are not only empowered with a flexible time frame for their units, but the number and kind of activities can be hand-picked from an extensive variety of options. This allows for the further customization of a program to the skill needs and general interests of the students, as well as the teaching style of the teacher.

Multiple teaching suggestions for every Core Word 1–1200 are included in ***Sourcebooks 2, 3,*** and ***4.*** Activities are listed for every high-use Core Word 1–1200. Teachers choose from among these activities to grow their classroom programs "their way" (see Article 17, page 71).

Where should a teacher begin instruction on the Core Word list?

Once the Core Words are divided by grade levels, it is recommended that teachers implement their program by beginning with the first few words on their list. Instruction begins with a research-based process that builds visual strategies for spelling and proofreading (see Article 4, page 21). Then the skill development follows with teachers choosing activities from the appropriate activity ***Sourcebook*** that lists activity options for each word.

How is review achieved?

Skills are recycled repeatedly within each grade level and from level to level. Previously introduced Core Words are also recycled again and again. This creates "built-in" review, creating an ongoing review process. Further, the ***Sourcebook*** *Reviews* provide more ongoing review. The *Reviews* are cloze and dictation activities for each set of five Core Words, as well as a careful recycling of previously introduced words. If teachers wish more review, they can note the previously introduced Core Words that recur in their invented form within students' everyday writing. These words can be added to any current Core Word unit.

Why is it unnecessary to regress instruction to the first Core Words to "catch up" to the grade-level Core Words and skills?

Because of this extensive review, it is unnecessary to start from "scratch" with Core Words and skill instruction. Upon initial implementation of the program, teachers should progress slowly through their grade-level Core Words, the ***Sourcebook*** skill-building activities, and ***Reviews*** that reinforce previously introduced Core Words and skills. This deliberate pace offers students the advantage of assimilating the built-in review of both words and skills introduced at earlier levels.

Because these Core Words serve as seeds for developing spelling and related skills and concepts, their presumed difficulty for spelling is immaterial. If a Core Word is deemed overly easy, teachers may eliminate it from the initial visual skill-building activity that commences each unit (see Article 4, page 21), however, the word can serve as a fine source for developing skills. For the word *arm,* students could be challenged through skill-building ***Sourcebook*** activities that include: exploring the multiple meanings and uses of *arm;* researching its other word forms, such as *armory, disarm, unarmed:* exploring idiomatic uses of *arm,* such as *up in arms;* looking at the plural *armies* and listing other words that follow this plural rule.

How were the words in the word bank within the frequencies 1000–1200 adjusted for upper grade-level students?

However, words 1000–1200 in the ***Spelling Sourcebook*** word bank (see Reference 1, page 77) have been edited for instructional appropriateness. Phonetically uncomplicated words with few letters have been omitted from the word bank within the frequencies 1000–1200. Instead, words with more instructional relevance are included in the word bank in their frequency-of-use order. This maintains program consistency.

What determined a word's grade placement in traditional spelling programs?

A spelling program that introduces words in frequency-of-use order is a major departure from traditional spelling methodology. In traditional programs, phonetic complexity was the main determiner of word placement. Phonetically complex words were included in the upper levels, while easier words filled the primary lists. A word's necessity for everyday writing had little to do with its grade placement. In fact, a high-use word that did not conform to the pattern or skill of a unit list may not have been included at all in the program.

What does research say about the best way to group words?

In contrast, the ***Spelling Sourcebooks*** call for a built-in bond between spelling and writing by ordering words for instruction by their frequency of use in writing. Research clearly states that the focus of spelling instruction should be on the high-use writing words to provide the greatest spelling facility for student writers.

This method of word placement eliminates words grouped by skills, such as letter sounds (play, train, game), structural patterns (bright, sight, light), or rules (baby/babies). Research does not report any long-term advantage to grouping words by these methods. In fact, patterned lists discourage long-term memory for mastery.

*How are the traditional skills included in the **Sourcebook** methodology?*

Yet, the concepts developed through the traditional word-grouping practices are worth learning. Students should know how sounds and spellings relate. They should learn to generalize spellings through patterned word families. Some spelling rules apply to a large number of words and have few exceptions. Such rules aid spelling accuracy. These and other traditional skills are included within the ***Spelling Sourcebook*** activity options (see Article 17, page 71). The Core Words serve as the seeds for their growth, as well as for the generation of additional words for exposure.

For example, a lesson in word patterns may develop as a result of the word *that* in the Core Word list (*hat, sat, mat, bat*). The Core Word *that* is the catalyst for introducing its rhyming family. Or the Core Word *same* might be the catalyst for students to brainstorm for words with other common spellings of the long *a* sound and collecting word examples for each (*ai, ay, a-consonant-e*). The Core Word *baby* may initiate a discussion of the *change-the-y-to-i-and-add-es* spelling rule (*baby/babies, lady/ladies, city/cities*).

How does the traditional presentation of skills differ from the Sourcebook approach?

So, all of the skills of the traditional programs are very much a part of the ***Spelling Sourcebook*** options for activities. The difference lies in the way in which the skills are generated. In the ***Spelling Sourcebook*** methodology, the skills emerge from high-frequency writing words as they appear in the Core Word lists. In the traditional programs, the skills were the centerpiece. The skills generated the words. The words provided the vehicle for practicing the skills. Another difference, and an important one, is that ***Spelling Sourcebook*** teachers decide which skills to teach and when, using an extensive resource of activity ideas available through ***Spelling Sourcebooks 2, 3,*** and ***4*** (see Article 17, page 71). Teachers select activities from these books to customize their programs. The traditional programs only offered the customizing option of skipping pages in a textbook. Further, unlike the traditional skill approach in which a specific skill was a one-time focus for a spelling unit, the ***Sourcebook*** methodology recycles the skills again and again to provide the opportunity for continuous exposure to expand students' understanding and application of the skills over time. Skills are introduced, practiced, applied, and reviewed through this ongoing approach to skill mastery.

Will the Core Words change from year to year?

Once the Core Words have been identified by grade level, a major part of the Core Curriculum has been created. The Core Words become the nucleus of the program. They provide the baseline content and the order in which the content is presented. The Core Words do not change over the years. They are the anchor from which a variety of language learning emerges.

Why might some teachers think their Core Words are too easy?

But one word of caution regarding these Core Words is necessary. It is not unusual for uninformed teachers to feel uncomfortable with the Core Words at first. They may say the words are too easy. They may say there are not enough words. They may want more words, harder words, providing rigor for the spelling test. These comments are indicators that these teachers may be confusing the ***Sourcebook*** Core Words with the word lists of old, traditional programs. In the old programs the words were the program and provided the rigor. The Friday Test provided a challenging assessment. Using the ***Sourcebook*** approach, the Core Words are not the total program and do not provide the rigor through assessment in isolation, apart from everyday writing.

How can the Sourcebook methodology ensure authentic instruction and assessment?

Again, spelling is not how many words a teacher covers, how hard the words are, nor how well the students spell the words on an isolated test of the words apart from writing. Spelling instruction must produce visible evidence of spelling competence *in writing* when random papers are selected for observation from across the curriculum (see Article 8, page 33, and Article 9, page 39). This ensures spelling authenticity—spelling aligned with real world use of spelling. Authentic spelling instruction and assessment rests on the interrelatedness of spelling and language skills applied within students' everyday writing across the curriculum (see Article 8, page 33, and Article 9, page 39).

Being sensitive to these teachers is the first step toward helping them develop confidence and competence using the new spelling instructional methodology, of which the Core Word lists are just one part. People operate within the parameters of their experience and current level of knowledge. And change is not easy for many people.

Nonetheless, for the program to be successful, it is critical for all teachers to fully understand and support its rationale. Support for the rationale develops only out of a clear understanding of it. Without this understanding, problems can incubate. One of the stumbling blocks within the spelling-for-writing methodology can often be traced to a misunderstanding of the appropriate roles of spelling words, reading words, and vocabulary words. To avoid this obstacle, read on.

Understanding the Differences:
Spelling Words, Reading Words, Vocabulary Words

Why can't most writers spell every word they can read?

The words you can read form a large word bank. The words you can spell form a smaller word bank. Generally, adult writers cannot spell every word they can read. The same is true of student readers and writers. Most second graders have a sizable number of words they can read, a few of which they can spell when they write.

Why is a reading word bank larger than a writing, or spelling, word bank? The answer is that reading is easier than spelling. Therefore, a reading word bank is more easily filled than a spelling word bank, and naturally results in a larger bank of words than the spelling bank.

Developmentally, reading is a skill that precedes the acquisition of spelling. Again, this is because it is easier to learn to read than it is to learn to spell. So, it follows that spelling words must be words that students have already learned to read.

Why are new reading words inappropriate spelling words?

Appropriate spelling words for students are the words that have the highest writing utility within their reading word bank. It is wasteful, perhaps even harmful, to attempt to teach students to spell words they cannot yet read with ease. It makes no sense to expect a student to learn to write the letter sequences of words that cannot be read once they are written. This expectation would be out of alignment with the normal developmental steps of language learning. Learning to read precedes learning to spell—and the acquisition of reading is more efficiently achieved through reading acquisition strategies rather than through the spelling acquisition strategies addressed in the ***Spelling Sourcebook*** methodology.

What are vocabulary words?

As students learn to read, most of the words they learn early on are words with which they are familiar. These words are part of their speaking and listening vocabularies. But as readers develop, they soon learn to read words for which they have little or no previous experience. These words are usually taught through a lesson related to the reading and are necessary for comprehending the reading material. Sometimes these words are somewhat technical, with applicability mainly within a narrow content area. Following the reading, students may be asked to write or discuss answers to questions that require them to use these new words to ensure that the words have been learned. These words are called vocabulary words and are taught through lessons that may be referred to as vocabulary development lessons.

Why are new vocabulary words inappropriate spelling words?

Learning new vocabulary words is important. Vocabulary development aids the thinking and learning process. The more words that can be understood, the greater the ability to think and learn. Yet, vocabulary words are not appropriate spelling words. Instead, spelling words must be words that students can already read and comprehend with ease. In contrast, vocabulary words are words with unfamiliar meanings that are just entering the reading word bank. They are new words.

This is not to say that reading skills and vocabulary cannot be reinforced through spelling instruction. They can. However, effective spelling instruction cannot accommodate new reading or vocabulary words within the Core Word list. Learning new reading and vocabulary words is important for language growth, but these words are inappropriate choices for spelling words.

How often do you need to use the word *photosynthesis* in everyday writing? A biologist or a science teacher may have cause to answer "often," but most people have not had the occasion to use the word since the last time they studied the topic.

Nonetheless, when students study plant life, *photosynthesis* is an important word. It is not, however, an appropriate Core Word for spelling. Core Words for spelling need to have long-term pertinence in writing. The word *photosynthesis* has pertinence only during the study of this scientific concept.

When is it reasonable to expect students to correctly spell new vocabulary words in their writing?

So, is it inappropriate for a biology teacher to expect students to spell the vocabulary word *photosynthesis* correctly on tests and papers that follow a unit of study on the topic? No, it is not inappropriate. Often a teacher *can* expect technical, low-frequency vocabulary to be spelled correctly in written assignments. However, with this expectation comes the need for instruction to ensure that the expectation can be met.

Prior to students beginning a writing piece that requires special words that are not high-frequency writing words, the class should brainstorm for these words. The words can be written on the chalkboard, the meanings reviewed, and the spelling skills discussed. For example, with the word *photosynthesis,* a likely point for skill discussion would be the *f* sound spelled with *ph.* Students might be asked later to collect other words that follow this sound/letter spelling pattern.

After the brainstorming session, the students are ready to write. The words generated during the brainstorming session can remain on the chalkboard as a spelling reference. However, if the writing is scheduled to be done another day or over a period of several days, a blackline-master spelling reference could be prepared with the words listed in alphabetical order. Indeed, with this instructional aid and the visual spelling reference, it is reasonable to expect students to spell and proofread technical vocabulary words correctly in their writing.

Why can't the Core Words constitute a total program?

In fact, literacy expects that writers know how to spell many words that go beyond a Core Word bank of 1200 high-use words. The Core Words are exactly what the name implies—the *core* program, or the nucleus. The Core Words are the foundation for a spelling program, but a complete spelling program requires expansion (see Article 12, page 51). Teacher-selected extension activities can introduce hundreds of additional words to students for exposure and discussion, so that students can make generalizations about their language and its correct use. Further, students must have the opportunity to add their own important words to complement the core program (see Article 11, page 49). These additional words come from the word banks of reading and vocabulary.

How are instructional priorities set for spelling?

However, in every curriculum priorities must be set. Everything cannot be taught. In the spelling curriculum, some words must be given a higher instructional priority than others. Spelling priorities are easier to set than priorities in most other curriculum areas because of the abundance of information collected on word frequencies in writing. Research on the frequency with which words are used in writing provides the basis for setting the priority that should be placed on the words for instruction.

For example, these studies clearly indicate that the vocabulary word *photosynthesis* is a lower-priority word than the thousands of words for which the likelihood of use in everyday writing is considerably greater. An example might be *because,* word number 127. This word will be needed often in everyday writing, so its priority is higher as a spelling word. Therefore, the priority "rating" of a word corresponds to its placement on a frequency-of-use list (see Reference 1, page 77). Word number 1 has the highest possible rating. As numbers increase, the priority decreases.

What is spelling mastery?

Educators are greatly challenged to ensure that students master the high-priority spelling words within the available time for spelling instruction. Mastery means spelling these words correctly with ease every time they are written. To achieve this, instructional emphasis must be placed on these high-use words rather than on lower-use vocabulary and reading words. Indeed, students are better served educationally having mastered a high-use bank of spelling words in their writing than having correctly spelled a lengthy list of vocabulary or reading words on a Friday Spelling Test . . . and promptly forgetting the spellings over the weekend.

Why might some teachers wish to include reading and vocabulary words on spelling word lists?

Nonetheless, some educators may be reluctant to relinquish the long lists of low-utility words for a spelling test. Why? One reason is that teaching new reading and vocabulary words for spelling instruction has been done for years. Though progress to abandon this tradition has been made, it is still fairly common for no instructional distinctions to be made among spelling words, reading words, and vocabulary words.

Another reason is that the inclusion of tricky, seldom-used reading or vocabulary words on the spelling list makes grading spelling objective and expedient. The test results often conform to the bell-shaped curve that can quickly be converted to percentages and recorded in a grade book. This neatly forms the data on which to make judgments regarding students' spelling abilities. Then the report card grade is based on this data, rather than on spelling in writing.

Over the years, has teacher training assisted teachers with the challenges of spelling instruction?

Obviously, re-education regarding spelling is the key. Most teachers genuinely want to be more effective, especially regarding spelling instruction. It's important to teachers to have their students spell well. However, teacher training has unfortunately provided little guidance toward this end. Some highly skilled master teachers say they've never had a course or staff development meeting offered to assist them with the challenges of teaching spelling.

A positive step toward more effectively teaching spelling is a commonsense definition of what spelling instruction is, its anticipated outcomes, and when it's mastered. Spelling is not "covering" words, but teaching students to spell in everyday writing. Words are never mastered until they can be spelled consistently correctly in writing.

Further, teachers need to feel comfortable making clear distinctions among reading words, vocabulary words, and spelling words . . . and subsequently emphasizing spelling words for spelling mastery. Research clearly supports the critical high-utility writing words for spelling mastery. Indeed, the higher the frequency of the word in writing, the sooner it should be mastered to provide the greatest support to a writer.

So, given a set of high-frequency writing words, what do teachers *do* with these words to ensure their mastery? Read on.

Using the Self-Corrected Test Procedure

The self-corrected test procedure is a multi-modality technique for learning to spell and proofread. The procedure is particularly strong for developing the dominant modality for spelling success, the visual modality. The effectiveness of the procedure lies with the teacher-guided self-correction of the words by each student. During the self-correction process, student attention is directed to each sequential letter of a word. This letter-by-letter method of observing words differs from the words-in-phrases method of seeing words for reading.

What is the purpose of a pretest?

The self-corrected test procedure is often referred to as the *pretest.* However, this procedure is not a test. It is a study technique. It outlines a *strategy* for learning to spell and proofread any word. Specifically, its purpose is to teach and practice the ability to visualize and write a familiar word from a long-term memory bank. This is essential for spelling and proofreading success.

Because the pretest is not a test, calling it a pretest may create misunderstanding. Because of the word *test* in its name, it would be easy to perceive the procedure as a test. If it is thought to be a test, words spelled correctly on this test may be interpreted as mastery of these words. However, spelling mastery occurs only when words are spelled consistently correctly in writing. In fact, calling the strategy-building process a test may not only encourage a misconception of its purpose, but can be counterproductive. Substituting the word *preview* for pretest prevents these possible problems. Following are three kinds of students who often benefit from substituting the word *preview* for pretest.

Why substitute the word preview for the word pretest?

Taking a spelling test produces anxiety in some students. When students feel stress, they are less receptive to incoming information. For these students, calling the pretest a preview of the words may help make the procedure a stronger study technique.

During the self-correction of a test, some students may feel uncomfortable revealing their errors and be eager to camouflage them. Removing the word *test* may encourage more students to follow the self-correction guidelines making the procedure a stronger study technique.

Finally, students who score 100% on a pretest may interpret this as having "passed the test." They may feel that no further requirement is necessary. Calling the pretest a preview discourages this misconception.

Which words are used on the preview?

The Core Words are used to teach and practice the visual skill-building process developed in the preview. It is the function of the Core Words to develop skills and concepts, so the grade-level Core Words provide the "seeds" for growing the skills associated with this strategy-building study process.

What materials are necessary for administrating a preview?

Students need paper and pencil for the preview. Regular writing paper can be used by folding the paper lengthwise in half, producing a "write" and a "rewrite" column. As an alternative to using regular writing paper, the Preview Blackline Master could be used (see Introduction to the Blackline Master, page 98).

Why should students print the words on the preview?

Students should *print* the words on the preview. It is far easier to form and retain a correct visual image of a word written in printing than in cursive handwriting. So, as students practice the preview process for learning to develop good spelling and proofreading habits, printing should be used.

If some teachers initially feel uncomfortable allowing their students to print, they should be reminded that printing is a lifetime skill. Printing should not be abandoned as soon as students are taught cursive handwriting. In fact, all forms and applications prominently request that the information be provided in printing, not cursive handwriting. So, having students print on the preview provides two clear advantages to the learner: First, it helps develop the habit of visualizing a word in printing; second, it affords an ongoing opportunity to maintain the lifetime skill of printing for special situations.

Should students study the words prior to the preview?

The purpose of the preview is to develop the ability to visualize a familiar word from a long-term memory bank. The high-frequency Core Words used on the preview are all familiar words. They are words with which students have had multiple experiences. Students can read the words with ease and may use the words in their everyday writing. So, students should not study the words prior to the preview. Instead, they should attempt to call these familiar words up into their mind's eye and write them from long-term, not short-term memory.

What is the procedure for administering the preview?

The steps for administering and correcting the preview need to be carefully demonstrated and monitored so that students apply the steps conscientiously and with confidence.

TEACHER	STUDENTS
Says the word. Says the word in a sentence. Says the word again.	Look at the teacher. Listen to the teacher.
Asks students to write the word.	Print the word in the left column of their paper.

What is the procedure for correcting the preview?

After the preview, students correct their own paper with teacher guidance, following these steps:

TEACHER	STUDENTS
Spells the word.	Proofread the word by touching each letter with the point of their pencil as the letter name is said. Circle errors.
Prints the word on the chalkboard, saying the name of each letter as it is printed.	Look at the chalkboard. Listen to the teacher.
Observes students.	Rewrite the word in the right column of their paper.

How many minutes does it take to administer and correct a preview?

The preview should be a brisk, structured activity. To make it efficient, students should be given precise expectations for the process. The teacher should set the rate of time the words are administered and corrected. Students must learn to listen and write the words competently. To encourage this, teachers should not repeat words nor allow for general discussion following the correction of each word. Instead, for the best results teachers should maintain a fast-paced, but comfortable administration and correction of the words.

Once this format is established, the time the process takes is minimal, depending upon how many words are presented on the preview. Few words, such as three to five, usually work better than more words. When too many words are presented, not only does the process become time-consuming, but ineffective. Some students take shortcuts and do not exert the effort to carefully visualize each word during the administration and may not copy words accurately during their correction.

How are errors identified during self-correction?

Circled word parts indicate errors. Students should not circle the whole word in which an error occurs. Instead, they should be asked to circle only the incorrect word part. This helps students see that the entire word is not incorrect, but that most of the letters are right. Then students should continue as well as they can to touch the remaining letters of the word as they are said by the teacher.

The correction procedure should always emphasize the correct spellings of the words in the "rewrite" column. Any incorrect word parts misspelled in the initial attempt to visualize the word and write it in the "write" column should not be the focus. So students need not feel the absolute necessity of circling precisely the omitted or incorrect letters. Rather, a bold circle merely indicates a problem area of the word. And the correction process should never review a misspelling to be certain that the circle was made in exactly the proper place of the word.

How should misspelled words in the "rewrite" column be handled?

During the correction of the preview, it should be made clear that it is the responsibility of the student to copy each word correctly into the "rewrite" column, the column on the right side of the paper. It can be explained that this necessitates looking at every letter the teacher writes and matching the letters, letter-for-letter in the word the student writes.

Each student's "rewrite" column needs to be checked. A small dot may be placed next to any misspelled word to indicate an error. Any misspelled words in this column should be corrected by the student. Misspelled words should not be corrected by another student, a teaching assistant, or the teacher. This would only delay a student's skill acquisition to accomplish the task independently.

Can all students be successful with the preview process?

Most students can, with some effort, be successful at following the guidelines for the preview. The words on the preview are familiar and the task is to visualize the words presented and write them from memory. Most of the words on the preview will be spelled by the students with accuracy on the initial writing in the "write"column. Students who have misspelled words in this column must take special care to spell the words accurately in the "rewrite" column from the teacher's model. If a student has difficulty with the process, then modifications can be made to ensure success until the student develops the prerequisite skills (see Article 13, page 53).

How does the review differ from the preview?

The preview introduces a unit of Core Words for a variety of skill development activities. The first skill developed with these Core Words takes place during the preview process. Specifically, visual skills are taught and practiced. Other language-integrated skills follow, such as exploring the other word forms of the Core Words or assembling a bank of words that follow the same spelling pattern of one of the Core Words (see Article 17, page 71).

A review closes a unit. The review has sometimes been referred to as the posttest. However, like the preview it is *not a test.* It is difficult not to equate the posttest with an assessment because spelling units have traditionally been brought to a close with a list test of the words that provides the students' spelling grades for the unit. However, the goal of spelling instruction is to transfer words to writing. So in a traditional posttest situation the grade is given before the goal has been reached. Of course, this is detrimental to achieving the goal at all!

The format for the review is flexible. Several alternative formats follow.

The review can repeat the preview process. This format is helpful to students who had difficulty on the preview. The words on the review can be exactly the same words that were presented on the preview. In this case, students know prior to the review which words they will be asked to write. This is a success-building format for students who experience a challenge in spelling. In some instances, teachers include a few previously introduced Core Words so that students can again activate their long-term memory banks to visualize the letters in the words.

Some teachers prefer to use another format for review. In addition to, or instead of a repeat of the preview, teachers review skills and concepts taught through the extension activities they chose to do during the unit. For example, if the unit included a lesson on the plural rules for vowel-y and consonant-y word endings, then the review might ask students to write the plurals for new words that illustrate this plural rule.

*What are the **Spelling Sourcebook Reviews**?*

Another format for the review employs the ***Sourcebook** Reviews.* The *Reviews* are cloze and dictation activities for a current set of five Core Words. Words that previously occurred in the word-frequency word bank are recycled through the cloze and dictation activities. The *Reviews* increase the actual review of words in the program, as well as provide a diagnostic tool for analyzing students' spelling facility of randomly selected words that occurred earlier on the frequency list. This format for a review cannot constitute an authentic spelling test because it does not test students' spelling in their everyday writing. Nonetheless, the *Reviews* provide a worthwhile activity that analyzes prerequisite spelling and usage skills toward their mastery.

What constitutes a real spelling test?

So the pretest, or the preview, and the posttest, or the review, are not real tests. The ***Sourcebook** Reviews* are not a real spelling test. A real test of spelling competency is how well a student spells and proofreads in writing (see Article 8, page 33, and Article 9, page 39, and Article 10, page 45). How can students be motivated toward real spelling competency? Read on.

Noting Student Spelling Progress

How does success affect learning?

Student motivation is an important component of effective learning. And success plays a key role in motivation—students who are successful are more motivated and thus learn more quickly and effectively. To aid spelling acquisition, especially for the reluctant speller, it is important to provide for and celebrate student success.

Using the ***Spelling Sourcebook*** methodology, students learn that they can spell. Particularly students who have been unsuccessful in traditional spelling instruction can be afforded a positive experience through a review of the Core Words that employs a format that repeats the preview. Performance expectations on the review are for all students to get all the words correct. As a result of this success, these students develop a new spelling confidence, as well as increased spelling motivation.

This is in sharp contrast to the Friday Test methodology characteristic of traditional spelling programs. This methodology produced a bell-shaped range of student performances based on the ability to memorize letter sequences of words. Often, many of these words had little relevance to everyday writing. On this test, some students were forced to the left side of the bell-shaped grading curve which clearly conveyed to them a message of failure.

What is the purpose of the progress chart?

Especially for students who are familiar with these feelings of failure, it is important to "showcase" the spelling success students achieve through the ***Spelling Sourcebook*** methodology. One of many ways to do this is through using a spelling progress chart. A chart can help students see that they are learning the recall process of spelling and proofreading success.

Who maintains the progress charts?

The progress charts are maintained by students, not the teacher. After each word preview, students record the number of words correct in the appropriate box on their spelling progress chart and set a personal achievement goal for their word review. The word review presents the same words as the preview. Following this review (on which students will generally score 100%), the number of words correct is again recorded on the chart. Spelling improvement is highlighted through the chart records. This evidence of success is motivating to students, particularly those for whom the development of spelling skills is difficult.

What role does the teacher play in successful use of the charts?

The teacher's role for effective utilization of the progress charts requires only minimum preparation time. The teacher should duplicate the charts on tagboard or a similar paper sufficiently substantial to remain intact over time, suggest a place for students to safely keep their chart, and provide time for the students to complete the chart following the preview and the review of the words. Further, the teacher can reinforce student success by discussing the information on the charts with students and complimenting their performance.

Is use of the progress chart required?

Use of the spelling progress chart is optional. However, especially for students who have had little success with spelling in the past, the benefits of using a progress chart can be dramatic. A visual record of progress can help motivate some students significantly, resulting in increased spelling growth. Further success-oriented activities are built into the ***Spelling Sourcebook*** methodology, such as students having access to the spelling words for which they are being assessed in their writing (see Article 8, page 33, and Article 9, page 39). Spelling success is key to continued spelling growth.

In fact, the overall success of the ***Sourcebook*** methodology can surely be contributed, in part, to the success students feel as they participate in the program. Students learn that spelling is achievable, which encourages a positive spelling consciousness. Now, how can students continue to learn to spell words on their own motivated by their new-found feelings of success with spelling? Read on.

Using the Independent Word-Study Procedure

What is the purpose of independent word study?

The independent word-study procedure is a multi-modality study strategy for learning to spell and proofread any word a writer wants to learn. Schooling cannot attempt to assume the responsibility for teaching students to spell every word they may need for writing over a lifetime. Instead, priorities need to be set for teaching those words that word-frequency studies indicate are more necessary than others in writing. Teachers should work to help students commit these words to their memory bank. Words that student or adult writers wish to add to this essential memory bank can be incorporated through the independent word-study procedure. This study process can be done throughout a lifetime of writing and learning.

How does independent word study differ from the study strategy employed in the preview process?

Essentially, the preview procedure and the independent word-study procedure share a common purpose. Both utilize a process that visually activates the memory bank for learning to spell and proofread familiar words. They differ in one main way. The preview process is teacher directed, while independent word study is learner directed.

How can students learn to use independent word study?

To familiarize students with independent word study, the teacher begins by demonstrating the procedure and having students practice it together. Once the steps in the procedure have been learned, students may use it independently, or in pairs, to learn to spell words. And to maintain correct use of the procedure over time, it may be necessary to review the steps of the procedure periodically.

When should independent word study be utilized?

This study technique can be used at any time to practice spelling and proofreading skills. It may be used following the preview for students who missed words. The independent word practice serves in this situation to provide an additional visual skill-building opportunity to call up the letter sequences of a familiar word. Some teachers have all students work through independent word study following the preview. According to the research on spelling acquisition, students who misspelled words on the preview should work through independent word study for the missed words until the words can be spelled accurately two times consecutively. Students who did not misspell words on the preview could complete their independent word study with one accurate practice of each word.

As the Priority Word list is expanded, additions could be practiced with independent word study (see Article 9, page 39). When students study words for their Individualized List, independent word study could be used (see Article 11, page 49). When parents want their children to learn to spell new words, such as the name of the city to which their cousins moved, the procedure could be used. Or anytime a student wants to learn to spell a word, the most efficient way to do so is through independent word study.

What are the five practice steps of independent word study?

The five practice steps are:

- **Read the word.**
  Students look at the word and say it aloud or silently.
- **Spell the word.**
  Students touch each letter with the point of their pencil and say the letter name, aloud or silently.
- **Cover the word.**
  Students cover the word, then form a visual image of the word from memory.
- **Print the word.**
  Students print the word.
- **Proofread the word.**
  Students uncover the word and check it letter for letter against the one they wrote.

This procedure can be practiced on regular student writing paper or on the Independent Word-Study Blackline Master (see Introduction to the Blackline Master, page 98). The blackline master lists the steps in the procedure as an aid during the study of
the words, and provides space for the practice of the words. If regular writing paper is used instead of the blackline master, the five study steps can be posted in the classroom as a visual reminder.

How are the preview procedure and the independent word-study procedure alike?

Both the preview procedure (see Article 4, page 21) and the independent word-study procedure are multi-modality *learning strategies.* These strategies provide the foundation for learning to spell and proofread *any* word. The Core Words that are employed within these procedures serve as "seeds" to grow the essential spelling and proofreading skills for lifetime spelling accuracy of all words used in writing.

What is the dominant learning modality for learning to spell and proofread?

The dominant learning modality in these two study strategies is the visual modality. The visual modality is the most critical for success in spelling and proofreading. But what about those students who have difficulty learning through the visual modality? Read on.

Developing Visual Skills

What is the dominant learning modality for spelling success?

Perhaps the biggest difference between writers who are challenged by spelling and those for whom the skill develops effortlessly is the ability to visualize. Though all learning modalities play a role in the acquisition of spelling skills, the visual modality is the dominant one.

Even for words that follow regular English spelling conventions, or rules, the visual modality is the most important for spelling success. The word *clean* is a regularly spelled word in the English language. Yet, it cannot be determined how *clean* is spelled by listening to the sounds of the letters when the word is said. Unfortunately, the English language does not have a high enough sound-to-symbol correlation to enable this to be done.

Instead, when the word is viewed in its written format, the viewer must note that the *k* sound is spelled with the letter *c, ea* is used to spell the long *e* sound, there is only one *n,* and there is no silent *e* on the end of the word. In fact, *clean* could be spelled *kleen,* or *klean,* or *klene,* or *kleanne,* or *cleen,* or *clene,* or *cleanne* . . . and still be perfectly "regular."

Knowledge of the language and its spelling rules cannot pinpoint the correct spelling of a word; it can only provide likely options. The only way to know which spelling option is the correct one is to remember. And the visual modality is the main key to remembering.

Can visual skills be taught and learned?

How, then, can instruction aid the ability to visualize? Indeed, some students may have great difficulty "seeing" a sequence of letters in their mind's eye to spell a word. These students may say they cannot see letters that are not really there. However, visualization can be learned. Learning to visualize can begin with students visualizing something they can see in their mind's eye, then building their visual skills from that point. For example, it is easier to visualize a circus elephant on its hind legs turning in circles than to visualize the letters in the word *clean.*

How can visualizing be explained to students?

To help students develop the ability to visualize, it is important that they know what *visualize* means. To explain *visualize,* students can be asked to pretend that they are looking at a large TV screen. Something is pictured on the TV screen. If the students say they see nothing on their screen, they should be asked to pretend they see something. Then they should describe what they see on their TV screen. What they see is called visualizing. It is seeing something that is not really there, but you pretend it is there.

What activities build visual skills?

Following are ten activities that can contribute to the general development of visual and recall skills.

1. Show students a picture. Ask them to observe it in detail for 30 seconds. Then ask students to write or tell everything they can remember about the picture. Next, give students an opportunity to look at the picture again and compare their descriptions with the picture.

2. Ask a student to stand in front of the class for 30 seconds. Then ask the student to go to the back of the room. Ask students to picture this person in their mind and tell or write what they see. Next, ask the student to step to the front of the class again. Compare the students' mind pictures with the real person.

3. Arrange several common objects inside a box with tall sides. Let students look into the box for a few seconds. Then ask students to tell or write what they remembered seeing. Next, review the items in the box. Compare what was remembered with what was there.

4. Ask students to describe in detail something with which they are familiar. Examples could include the school office, the kitchen in their home, or the front of their house or apartment building. Then have students compare the description with the real thing.

5. Place a few familiar objects in a dark plastic garbage bag and tape it shut. Then ask students to feel the objects to try to identify them. Next, have the students tell or write what they think is inside the bag. Last, check the contents of the bag.

6. Play an instrumental piece of music. Ask the students to write or tell what they think might be taking place in a movie when this music accompanies the action.

7. Have students pretend that they will be granted a wish for a new "dream" room, or car, or outfit of clothing. Then have students tell or write a description of what they were granted.

8. Ask students to tell or write directions of how to get from one place to another within the school—for example, how to get from their classroom to the gymnasium. Then ask pairs of students to follow one another's directions to determine the accuracy of the directions.

9. Read a visual description of a place or person the students know. Ask them to identify what or who it is.

10. Show students a shape or design drawn on a large card. Ask the students to study it and create a mental picture of it. Then have them draw what they recall seeing. Begin with easy shapes and designs, such as a circle with an *x* inside. Progress to more complex formations. Then, include high-use writing words the students would benefit by knowing how to spell.

Once students have participated successfully in activities that develop general visual and recall skills, they can be challenged to activate their visualizing skills to see short words and their letters.

How can a "spelling screen" aid spelling acquisition?

A short, easy-to-read word can be printed on the chalkboard, then erased. The students should look at the board and try to visualize the word still being there. Next, the students can try looking in a direction away from the chalkboard and visualizing the word on their TV screen. This is their "spelling screen."

Students should experiment with visualizing by picturing the words printed on their spelling screen larger, smaller, or a different color. Students can be asked to "read" the letters in the words on their spelling screen and then, write the letters in the words just as they appear on their screen.

Students should use their spelling screen to recall the letters in a word whenever they need to spell words. They should be encouraged to activate their spelling screen when they write words for the self-corrected Core Word previews and reviews (see Article 4, page 21), when they use the independent word-study procedure (see Article 6, page 27), when they play spelling games, when they write, and when they proofread.

What benefits can be attributed to the ability to visualize?

The ability to visualize has benefits beyond spelling acquisition. Reading and listening comprehension is enhanced when a student can easily visualize the characters and action in a story as it's being read or told. The ability to organize is preceded by a visual accounting of the steps necessary to reach a desired outcome.

And, of course, visualizing "success" has been validated as an ingredient that often sets "winners" apart from "losers." Students need to develop the ability to visualize themselves as spelling winners! Indeed, the ability to visualize can contribute to student achievement in a variety of positive ways.

But the ability to visualize alone will not necessarily result in spelling mastery. Another important element must be instilled in the students' approach to spelling. This element is *accountability*. For more on accountability and its role in spelling acquisition, read on.

Developing Accountability for Spelling in Writing

What are six ingredients for a successful spelling-for-writing program?

Spelling accuracy in writing can be taught and learned. The ingredients for achieving spelling and proofreading proficiency include:

1. Emphasizing spelling mastery of high-use *writing words,* not new reading or vocabulary words
2. Defining spelling *mastery* as accurate spelling and proofreading in everyday writing, not just on a spelling test
3. Structuring instruction for *success,* not failure
4. Utilizing *research-based* learning strategies, including the self-corrected test and independent word-study procedure
5. Providing guidance for enhancing the *visual* learning modality

Beyond these high-priority elements, the degree to which spelling and proofreading accuracy can be achieved in everyday writing is dependent upon one significant factor . . . *accountability.*

What are the steps for building a foundation for spelling accountability?

How can teachers make students accountable for spelling correctly in everyday writing? Before accountability can be achieved, a foundation must be established. First, a need, or purpose, for the desired learning must be established. All learning is more effective when the learner sees a purpose for the learning.

Second, goals, or learning expectations, must be set. At the same time, the skills necessary for successfully meeting the expectations must be taught and practiced.

Third, what is "expected" must be "inspected." The inspection provides data for yet another important component of spelling and proofreading success—performance feedback. Efficient teaching requires frequent opportunities for giving performance feedback to communicate the students' current level of achievement toward meeting the expectations. And, of course, the degree to which the expectations are being achieved is often translated into evaluations, or student grades. Thus, accountability!

Establish a Purpose for the Learning	+	Set Goals	+	Provide Instruction & Practice	+	Furnish Performance Feedback	=	Accountability

How can a purpose for learning to spell be established?

How do teachers help students see the purpose for spelling conventionally? Establishing a purpose for learning to spell begins early on. Students need to learn that spelling is important. Spelling is a courtesy to the reader and clearly an aid to communicating literately.

Even beginning writers can relate to the challenges of deciphering spelling approximations as they struggle to read each others' first stories. They can see the advantages of having one right way of spelling—a system that everyone learns and uses. The primary students can have fun picturing the confusion of trying to read the morning newspaper in a country that had no such system.

For post-primary students, the absolute necessity of using conventional spellings for business writing can be repeatedly and vigorously substantiated. But business is for adults, and adulthood is a ways away for these students. This information, often in the form of warnings, rarely provides a level of student motivation sufficient to ensure that students accept the responsibility for their spelling. So, establishing a clear purpose for learning is important, but not enough to ensure accountability.

What factors need to be considered as spelling goals are set?

The degree of motivation generated by purpose must be increased by clear goals and expectations. Yet, developing student writers cannot be expected to spell all words correctly every time they write. If they were, few would write. Many of a beginning writer's words should be accepted with approximate spellings, just as a very young child's approximations of pronunciation are expected and accepted when he or she is learning to talk. However, a time comes when the baby talk should diminish and the child should progress to conventional ways of saying words. Likewise, beginning writers must show progress in acquiring the ability to produce conventional spellings in everyday writing (see Article 16, page 67).

But what constitutes realistic spelling expectations, or goals? Some of the answers can be found by examining the expectations set for reading. Reading is an area in which most educators have expertise. A comparison between reading and spelling will provide the basis for making decisions regarding expectations and accountability for spelling.

How are reading and spelling mastery alike?

What is a good reader? Is it someone capable of decoding words with accuracy when the words are flashed on word cards? No. Reading is more than isolated word calling. Good readers are expected to read words in context, not just on word cards. They are expected to read for meaning. The act of reading in context and understanding what is read is a very important part of reading instruction and practice. Indeed, reading mastery is the reader's ability to understand what is read in context. So, reading instruction goes well beyond simply decoding independent words. Instead, the expectation, or goal, for reading is that the reader will understand the words being read. The reader must be able to understand the message the writer wrote.

The same is true of spelling. A good speller can spell words in isolation, but can also spell words within the context of writing. Therefore, all conscientious spelling instruction and practice goes beyond spelling words with accuracy in isolation on a Friday Spelling Test, apart from writing. Instruction must include the expectation that words will be accurately spelled within the context of writing. So, spelling mastery, like reading mastery, must be based on developing the ability to perform in context. The expectation, or goal, for the writer is to use conventional spellings in writing, making the message easily communicated to the reader. And this requires proofreading.

What is the difference between a minor spelling oversight and a spelling error?

Proofreading and spelling are bonded, inseparable. If a word is misspelled in final-copy writing, it is an error. Even when the word could be easily spelled on a spelling test, if it is misspelled in writing . . . it is *wrong.* The careless proofreading errors of student writers are sometimes dismissed by teachers as minor editing oversights. Teachers know that the students could spell these words if asked to on a spelling test, so they do not consider the errors a spelling deficiency.

Indeed, this attitude significantly contributes to the current state of spelling illiteracy in writing. It teaches students that spelling does not "count" in writing. Yet, the world outside the classroom does not share this opinion. Because the expectation, or goal, for spelling is to spell well *in writing,* surely some misspellings in writing must "count."

What are spelling expectations for final copies in the writing process?

So, which words in writing "count" for spelling? This depends upon the purpose for the writing. If the purpose for the writing is to practice the process, or stages, through which writing progresses toward a "published" work, then students should produce an error-free final copy. Spelling feedback can be provided within the stages along the way. But students should be made fully aware that they are accountable for spelling and using all words correctly in their final copy. For writing pieces developed through the writing process, spelling accountability should be 100% accuracy for every word.

Why do spelling expectations differ for final copies in the writing process and for writing in everyday assignments?

However, everyday assignments that require writing do not progress through several drafts like the writing that is a part of the multi-draft writing process. So, spelling expectations for student writers in everyday writing should not be as high as for writing that is part of an ongoing process that produces a writing piece over time through many revisions.

Yet, developing writers *should* be made accountable in their everyday writing for the words that research indicates are used most often in writing. It makes good sense to hold students accountable for an increasing number of these words in their everyday writing before holding them accountable for lower-frequency words.

For example, a student should sooner be held accountable for the word *they,* than for the word *teacher* because *they* occurs more often in writing than *teacher.* This allows for the most rapid and efficient progress toward error-free spelling in writing. The words for which students are first made accountable are the words that occur most often in their everyday writing, now and throughout their life.

Selecting words for accountability in everyday writing is similar to a game of chance based on probability. If a fine prize could be won for predicting the color of the next car passing City Hall, it would be wise to choose a very common car color. If research indicates that over half the cars in the city are blue, there is a greater likelihood that the next car passing City Hall will be blue than there is that it will be any other color. Choosing blue would therefore provide the best possible chance to win the fine prize.

Which words provide the most mileage toward spelling literacy?

If another fine prize is offered to teachers for developing student writers who spell well on random samples of everyday writing, it would be wise to help the students master the words that research indicates are the most commonly used in everyday writing. The occurrence of the high-use words *they, because, until,* or the homophones *their/there/they're* or *to/too/two* in a randomly selected writing sample is more likely than the occurrence of *photosynthesis.* Choosing to emphasize the mastery of high-frequency writing words would provide the best possible chance to win the fine prize. At the same time, it would provide for the greatest growth in spelling literacy for students.

What is a priority word?

So, it's the high-use writing words for which students should be made accountable for spelling correctly in their everyday writing. These words are the students' Priority Words. They are the first words consecutively occurring on the frequency-of-use list (see Reference 1, page 77). They are not Core Words. Core Words and Priority Words are necessarily different banks of words.

Where do the Core Words and Priority Words occur on a frequency-of-use master word list?

For example, a group of sixth graders may progress through Core Words with the frequencies 700–900 over their sixth-grade school year. However, these sixth graders cannot realistically be held accountable at the end of the year for spelling all words with frequencies 1–900 correctly every time they write. This is true even if these sixth graders spelled every one of these 900 Core Words correctly on the Core Word previews and reviews beginning with their first set of words in grade one.

These same sixth graders may be asked to be accountable for Priority Words up to the frequency of 125. This means that words 1–125 make up their Priority Word list. These Priority Words, which the sixth graders must spell correctly in their everyday writing, were Core Words in grades one and two.

How are Core Words and Priority Words different?

The Core Words are the words that are the "seeds" assigned to each grade level for "growing" a program rich with skills and concepts on the students' *instructional level.* They provide a vehicle for learning the visual strategies that dominate the practice labeled earlier as the Core Word preview. They also provide the catalyst for "springboarding" to related language activities which build experiences with hundreds of additional words.

Are students accountable for spelling Priority Words with accuracy?

In contrast, the Priority Words are well below the students' *instructional* level on a frequency-of-use list. They are words on the students' *independent* writing level. The students are responsible for spelling their Priority Words correctly in everyday writing for every teacher, in every subject—these words are no longer acceptable in their invented form. They are the "no excuses" words. Their purpose is to develop spelling accountability in writing. The Priority Word list sets the level for which spelling literacy must not fall below in a classroom—it is the baseline for spelling accountability. Mastery is *expected* for these words *all the time,* not most of the time.

Are students accountable for spelling Core Words?

But, Core Words cannot be expected to be mastered following their appearance in an instructional unit. Students should spell the Core Words correctly in all the Core Word activities and, as the unit is brought to a close, spell the words correctly on the review activity. This review is not mastery. Mastery takes place over time. This is achieved through ongoing everyday writing in which students are encouraged, but not required, to spell their Core Words correctly. Further, the Core Words are reviewed extensively within the activities of ***Spelling Sourcebooks 2, 3,*** and ***4*** as subsequent Core Words are introduced. They are reviewed again and again through the ***Sourcebook Reviews,*** the blackline master cloze activities and dictation sentences. Teachers may expand this built-in review by selecting review Core Words that students often misspell for recycling on a subsequent word preview. This abundant review provides far greater mastery of the Core Words than the mastery of the traditional word-list words, all of which promptly vanished following the Friday Test.

What are appropriate expectations for spelling in writing?

The goal, then, for spelling in writing is to spell and proofread with accuracy all words on the final copy of writing that is done through the writing process. These words would include Priority Words, Core Words, and all other words. In everyday writing, the spelling goal is to spell the Priority Words (and any added technical words) consistently correctly. A reasonable number of Priority Words needs to be established (see Article 9, page 39), and then the basic expectation is for students to proofread for these words in all of their everyday assignments that require writing. Further, if students have been given a reference list of technical vocabulary words pertinent to a specific writing topic, these words are also expected to be spelled with absolute accuracy (see Article 3, page 17). Of course, students should be expected to grow in spelling accuracy in writing beyond the Priority Words and technical reference words, but to many words including some Core Words. A top spelling grade should be awarded only to students who exceed the basic expectation (see grading, Article 10, page 45).

What skills are necessary for learning to spell and proofread?

Once the purpose for spelling has been addressed and spelling accountability in writing clearly stated, the skills for achieving this accountability must be taught and practiced. Students must be taught how to look at words differently for spelling and proofreading than they look at words for reading. This is learned through the ***Spelling Sourcebook*** Core Word previews, the independent word-study procedure, springboard activities that build visual skills, and through students' constant proofreading of Priority Words in their everyday writing. Spelling and proofreading within writing constitutes the *application of spelling skills.* And it is the mastery of the application of spelling that is the goal of all spelling instruction.

Why is the transfer of spelling to writing a challenge?

Yet, the greatest challenge over the years in teaching students to spell lies in the disappointing results of students' attempts to transfer their spelling words to writing.

Why can't students spell high-use words correctly in writing? The answer is that they don't have to in the traditional curriculum. And they know it. The goal for spelling has been defined for students as spelling well on a Friday Test. It is this test that is inspected for correct spellings. It is this test that provides the performance feedback to the students on spelling competence. And it is this test that determines the spelling grade. So, students know that this test is the most important thing in spelling. It is no coincidence that asking students to proofread for spelling in their writing holds little interest for them.

What changes need to take place to ensure the transfer of spelling to writing?

Teacher verbiage stating that the new goal of spelling is to spell well in writing won't change anything . . . until the importance of the Friday Test is completely supplanted by spelling in writing. To ensure the transfer of spelling to writing, writing must be regularly inspected. Most students, and adults, make an effort to do what is "expected" and "inspected." Then, it follows that student writing, not the test, should provide the format for the performance feedback. And it follows that the level of spelling achievement in writing, not the test, should provide the basis for the spelling grade (see Article 10, page 45). Indeed, spelling *in writing* must be redefined as *the test.*

From what source is data gathered to provide performance feedback on spelling the Priority Words?

The data for the performance feedback on correct spelling and use of the Priority Words must be gathered from randomly selected writing assignments. To promote success on these random inspections, the Priority Words should be made available to students in the form of an alphabetized personal spelling reference list. Then, while students write, the Priority Word list can be used as a resource to confirm the correct spellings for which the students are accountable.

But are students really mastering the Priority Words if they can check their spellings on a spelling reference list? Regular assessments without the reference list are useful (see Article 15, page 63); however, using available resources for writing should be encouraged. Such spelling references are not prohibited in real-life situations, so they should not be prohibited at school in an authentic curriculum.

Why should use of a reference list for the Priority Words be encouraged?

All writers, adults as well as students, need to learn to habitually use resources that enable them to produce a better written product. Therefore, it is appropriate for students to regularly use their Priority Word reference list to confirm spellings. It is inappropriate not to use the reference if there is a question about spelling accuracy. In fact, repeated checkings and writings of the Priority Words increase the rate of mastery of these high-frequency words, so that eventually students can spell the words correctly in writing without a reference as easily as they spell their own names.

How do expectations for Priority Words change?

As students make progress mastering their Priority Words, expectations, or goals, should be increased in accordance with their progress. For example, the Priority Word list at the beginning of a school year may be the first 30 high-frequency words for a specific group of students. Then, as soon as the students demonstrate proficiency spelling and proofreading all of these words in their everyday writing, the list could be increased, perhaps to 35 words. The five additional words are the next five words that occur consecutively on the frequency-of-use word list. By the end of the school year, the number of Priority Words for which the students are accountable will be considerably greater than at the beginning of the school year.

So, Priority Words increase in number over a school year. They also increase for a particular grade level over a period of years. For example, suppose that a certain school begins the school year using the spelling-for-writing methodology, and a fifth-grade class of students is held accountable for 42 Priority Words at the beginning of this school year. Four years from now, the same expectation for the incoming fifth graders may be far too low because the teachers in grades one through four have already been expecting accountability for the spelling of these words in the students' everyday writing. The students will have risen to the level of achievement for which they have been made accountable.

How are achievement and accountability related?

Accountability, then, is an essential component of spelling literacy in writing. It is achieved through stating a purpose for the learning, setting expectations, providing instruction and practice, making inspections to provide performance feedback, and furnishing subsequent evaluations of the students' achievement. Traditional spelling programs have been sadly lacking in accountability. Without clearly establishing accountability for spelling in writing, no spelling program can produce results in student writing.

It's the Priority Words that take center stage for accountability for spelling in everyday writing. How is an appropriate expectation for Priority Words established, and exactly how can the words be regularly checked for correct use in writing? Read on.

Establishing Priority Words and Checking for Their Accuracy in Writing

Priority Words are the words for which students are accountable for spelling correctly in all of their everyday writing, for every teacher, in every subject (see Article 8, page 33). How can an appropriate list of these words be established for students?

Why is the selection of Priority Words based on spelling in writing instead of spelling on a test?

Selecting the Priority Words is always a judgment call, but with experience and cooperative discussion among teachers, the judgments can be made fairly easily. However, the judgment must always be based on observations of students' spelling on everyday writing assignments. It cannot be based on any test of the words in isolation, apart from writing. This is because mastery of spelling words can only be determined through writing, not from a words-in-isolation spelling test. Often students can spell words on a test, but cannot spell or proofread for the words within the context of their own writing.

What kind of writing samples are appropriate for determining Priority Words?

To determine how many Priority Words would be suitable to hold students accountable for in their everyday writing, random samples of writing need to be collected from all students. These writing pieces should be everyday writing assignments, not drafts or final copies from writing-as-a-process assignments.

Papers that are a part of the writing process progress through several stages of revision toward the final copy. During the writing process, the writer should not be held accountable for any spelling on the first draft, but should be held accountable for the spelling of *all* words on the final copy. The final copy must be free from error.

In contrast, everyday writing assignments are papers that do not progress through multiple stages of refinement. Instead, they are written, proofread, turned in to the teacher, generally checked for content, and then returned to the writer. Everyday writing assignments are any assignments that require writing, except writing-as-a-process pieces. They might include the written answers to the questions at the end of the social studies chapter, the daily weather report, a predicted ending for a story being read aloud to the class, or a brief summary of a science experiment in science class.

The misspelled words and misused homophones on these randomly selected everyday writing samples reveal which words the students have not yet mastered. Even if the errors are words that the students would surely spell correctly on a spelling test, they are errors.

What information is collected from these writing samples?

As errors are identified, it should be noted where on the frequency-of-use word list they occur. Some teachers may choose to keep a tally of the errors as they read the papers. This can be facilitated by using the list of the high-frequency words (see Reference 1, page 77) or by employing one of the Record Keeper Blackline Master (see Introduction to the Blackline Master, page 98). Of course, attention should be focused on errors in the higher-frequency words, because the errors on lower-frequency words are not a priority until the higher-frequency words are mastered.

Once this information has been collected, how many Priority Words the students will have on their list can be determined. Again, this is a judgment call. The list should encompass a few words students are misspelling in their writing, but not too many.

Why are words selected for a Priority Word list in the order of their frequency of use?

A Priority Word list for students consists of word number 1 (*the*) on the frequency-of-use list (see Reference 1, page 77) consecutively through to whatever number of words has been determined to be appropriate. If 25 is the number of words determined to be appropriate for a Priority Word list, the list includes word number 1 (*the*) through word number 25 (*have*). The 25 words are in no way randomly selected words, but a subsection of the frequency-of-use list. This is to ensure that students are held accountable for the highest-use words before they are held accountable for words that are not as critical in everyday writing.

To explain, the following information was generated from 79 everyday writing samples gathered at the beginning of the school year from a class of 28 fourth graders. There were about 3 one-page samples per student. This data provided the basis for determining the Priority Words for this class, with the exception of two Special Needs students for whom the Core Word program and Priority Word list were modified (see Article 13, page 53). Among the first 100 high-frequency words, these errors were made—

word	frequency	# of different students making error
of	2	1
to	5	9
are	15	2
they	19	5
were	34	3
there	37	15
which	41	2
their	42	12
said	43	1
then	53	2
many	55	1
would	59	2
could	70	1
than	73	5
first	74	3
been	75	2
its	76	6
only	85	2
little	92	3
where	98	2

This group of students made frequent errors on the homophones *there* and *their.* Usage was also the culprit with these words: *to, are, then, than,* and *its.* These homophone errors reflect inaccurate spellings for the words the writers intended to

How might students perform on a word list test of their Priority Words?

use. Indeed, many of the errors indicated on the chart would not occur as errors if the students were given a traditional test of the words. But, if words are not spelled and used correctly in writing, they have not yet been mastered.

Perhaps an appropriate Priority Word judgment for this class would be to begin with words 1–36, or words *the* through *when* on the frequency-of-use list. These words would be the baseline of spelling literacy and be unacceptable in their invented form.

The word *there* (number 37) is a significant problem among these students. When *there* is added, it necessitates differentiating among all three homophones: *there, their,* and *they're.* Context sentences for easy reference for their correct use should be provided. Teachers might circle any of these misused homophones in students' everyday writing for approximately three weeks in preparation for their addition to the Priority Word list. Once added, these homophones are unacceptable to misspell or misuse on any piece of everyday writing.

A Priority Word expectation must be clearly stated. Then to ensure that the expectation is taken seriously by the students, teachers must maintain high standards for meeting the expectation. The words *cannot* be misspelled or misused, or something less than a "satisfactory" spelling grade is earned.

Though students made additional spelling errors on words beyond the top 36 on the frequency-of-use scale, those words are not as critical for mastery at this time as the words that occur prior to word 36.

What problem could result from too many words being included on a Priority Word list?

Initially, the Priority Word expectation should allow students to be successful early on. Then the number of Priority Words can be increased in regular, small increments. This is better than beginning with too rigorous an expectation. When too many words are included on the Priority Word list, expectations may exceed what students can meet. This may retard writing production, as well as foster feelings of anxiety or failure. It may also encourage a relaxed attitude toward the expectation. If a goal is set too high, it is often disregarded. To avoid these pitfalls, teachers should begin with a realistic expectation, then add more words as soon as progress is noted.

If students exhibit particular difficulty with the mastery of some Priority Words, mini-lessons might aid their mastery. Occasional instructional help with tricky homophones may be appropriate. But, once the expectation is set, the responsibility is on the student to strive to meet the goal independently.

How are words added to a Priority Word list?

More words should be added to the Priority Word list as mastery of the original words is noted, choosing the next few words consecutively from the frequency-of-use list. The list is always cumulative. Once students are made accountable for a word, they remain accountable indefinitely as they develop as writers. This ensures steady spelling progress in writing, with no opportunity to revert to irresponsible spelling habits as writers grow and develop through the grades.

As words are added to the Priority Word list, it is not necessary to pretest the words. Nonetheless, as words become Priority Words, teachers may suggest that students study the new words using their independent word-study procedure (see Article 6, page 27).

How are words with frequencies between the Priority Words and Core Words included for instruction?

Words that are often misspelled or misused in everyday writing, but fall between the Priority Words and the Core Words on the frequency-of-use list, can be added to selected Core Word units. For example, a group of students may have words 1–75 as Priority Words, be currently working on Core Words 612–618, but make frequent errors in their everyday writing on *because,* word 127. *Because* could be added to a Core Word unit for study. Further, if the teacher deems *because* to be used so frequently in students' writing, it may then be added out of sequential order to the Priority Word list.

Why may Priority Words be different for students in the same grade?

As teachers at the same grade level are establishing their Priority Word lists, some consistency should be reflected in their expectations. However, it is possible for two different third grades to have different expectations for Priority Words if one group's everyday writing exhibits a higher level of spelling proficiency. It is also possible to set different expectations within the same classroom to accommodate different student abilities. Teacher discussion and cooperative judgments should be encouraged so that the best decisions are made for all students.

Once the Priority Words have been determined, the students need to be provided with an alphabetical list of the words to use for reference. The list can be duplicated on heavy-weight paper that is sturdy enough to remain intact with daily use. The Priority Words may also be posted in the classroom. Some teachers provide a homophone reference for the Priority Word homophones. This could be included on the same reference that lists the Priority Words, on a separate paper, or on classroom posters. The homophone reference can provide easy-to-read context sentences for differentiating between tricky homophones.

Why should students be encouraged to use a list of their Priority Words as a spelling reference?

Students should be vigorously encouraged to use all available spelling and usage references for their Priority Words (see Article 8, page 33). They are accountable for these words in all their writing. Student writers must learn that it is unacceptable not to use references if they have any doubt about accuracy of the words for which they are accountable. This is an expectation that society holds for adult writers, and students will benefit by learning to meet that expectation as they learn to write.

How can the Priority Word list be modified when it becomes too long for easy reference?

Teachers in the junior high/middle school grades and elementary teachers with very capable writers will eventually have students who are accountable for many Priority Words. To make the students' Priority Word reference more efficient, teachers may want to shorten it by eliminating words for which a spelling reference is no longer necessary (*the, and, it, in,* etc.). Nonetheless, the students always remain accountable for the complete list which can be posted in the classroom as a reminder.

Students should be clearly informed of the expectations for Priority Words—that the words must always be spelled and used correctly in all of their everyday writing assignments. No excuses. And students must understand that their spelling grade depends upon their spelling performance in these assignments (see Article 10, page 45).

How are writing samples selected for Priority Word feedback on spelling accuracy?

With concise expectations set, random inspections of students' everyday writing can begin. The papers randomly selected for noting spelling progress should be everyday assignments. They should not be drafts of writing-as-a-process assignments. If various teachers share the educational responsibility for students, *all* teachers must cooperate. If necessary, the language arts or English teacher should occasionally ask for writing samples for a few students from a content-area teacher to alert the students that spelling accountability does not begin and end with their language arts or English class.

One everyday writing assignment can be selected from every student every week, or as often as possible. English or language arts teachers teaching several classes of students who have many Priority Words cannot be expected to meet this suggestion. However, the more often students are provided with feedback, the more rapidly their spelling improves. Students should not be told which papers will be selected, but they should know that any paper they write could be chosen. Teachers can choose a variety of writing pieces from different students. A few students' papers can be selected on Monday, a few Tuesday . . . and so on through a week, making it difficult for students to predict when one of their papers might be chosen. This will encourage students to strive to spell their Priority Words with accuracy on all their everyday written assignments.

Should the feedback include only errors on Priority Words?

If teachers wish, they can mark errors other than misspelled Priority Words on the papers they select for correction. In addition to Priority Word errors, technical reference words should be marked if students were provided with a reference for these words (see Article 3, page 17). Other errors could be noted, but students must not be penalized for using interesting words with unfamiliar spellings. This would stifle creativity and vocabulary growth.

How long should writing samples be?

To be time-effective, an entire writing piece need not be assessed. Only a paragraph or a few lines can be inspected on each writing sample. Brackets in the margin of the paper can designate the writing assessed for spelling. Though the spelling expectation for students is for "every day all day long," brief writing samples routinely selected at random can clearly convey the message that a teacher cares, and *is looking.*

As teachers mark students' papers, they should increasingly place the responsibility for editing on the student by choosing a marking method that requires students to learn the skills for being their own personal editor. Teachers can develop their own system for checking these papers, or they can adopt or adapt one of the following methods.

How can writing samples be marked for performance feedback on Priority Words?

1. Write the Priority Word errors at the bottom of the paper.
2. Write the Priority Word errors at the bottom of the paper and, as further aid, place a dot in the margin of the paper to indicate on which writing line a mistake occurred.
3. Place a dot in the margin to indicate on which writing line a mistake occurred.

4. Place a numeral on the paper to indicate the number of Priority Word errors that were made. (If it is initially too difficult for students to find their own errors, introduce the method by asking them to find their errors cooperatively with a partner.)
5. Write the errors on a sticky-note and attach it to the paper.
6. Underline or circle the Priority Word errors.
7. Use highlighter pen to discreetly signal Priority Word errors.

What are students' responsibilities regarding Priority Words?

After the checking, the writing papers should be returned to the students. The students are responsible for correcting their errors. They do not need to rewrite the entire assignment, just correct the errors indicated. Next, the students can return their corrected papers to the teacher or check the corrections with a designated student or teaching assistant.

To maintain a positive classroom atmosphere, it is important for teachers to be generous with praise when evidence suggests that students are making progress mastering the Priority Words. The Priority Words need to be a *positive* "high priority" in the classroom. The focus should be on success, rather than on mistakes. To ensure this success, teachers should set realistic expectations, engage in regular and random inspections, and "showcase" *success* to generate the positive feelings associated with achievement.

How will parents accept the concept of Priority Words?

Also important to the success of any new curriculum is inclusion of the parents. Parents need to be informed of upcoming spelling curriculum changes and the reasons for them (see Article 14, page 59). In introducing the ***Spelling Sourcebook*** methodology, it will be particularly important to explain to parents the role of the Priority Words. Parents will need to understand that their child's spelling grade reflects how the child spells and uses the Priority Words in everyday writing. This is a change parents will gladly embrace . . . they *want* their child to spell well in written assignments. They want visible evidence in their child's writing that their child is learning to spell. Parents are uncomfortable with misspellings in writing. And the role of the Priority Words is to place the highest priority on learning to correctly spell high-use words in writing.

How do Priority Words relate to spelling evaluation?

Students' spelling of the Priority Words in their everyday writing forms the basis for determining their spelling grade. However, other factors are also involved in grading. To learn more about the evaluation process, read on.

Article 10

Grading Spelling Progress

How do grades reflect educational priorities?

Should a student's report card include a grade for spelling? Some school districts have diminished the prominence of grading in general, and one of the first grades to be removed from the report card was the grade for spelling.

However, in most schools, grades or performance evaluations are still a fact of life. Evaluations reflect educational priorities . . . for better or for worse. What is graded, is perceived to be important. So, if spelling well is a high priority, spelling should have the same evaluative status as any other important subject.

What should the main factor be in determining a spelling grade?

For evaluation to be authentic and effective, it must always be tied to the learning goal. The learning goal for spelling can be simply stated: spelling and proofreading well in writing. Clearly, the main factor in determining the spelling grade must therefore be a student's ability to spell and proofread *in writing*. This emphasis convincingly affirms the learning goal for spelling and provides the foundation for authentically evaluating a student's progress.

Why do most students think that the goal for spelling is high performance on the Friday Spelling Test?

Currently, most students believe that spelling well on the Friday Spelling Test is the learning goal for spelling instruction. Why? Performance on this test determines all or most of the students' spelling grades. The criteria for the grade sets the perceived goal.

A class experiment can verify this. Students can be given the choice of having one of two wishes granted. First wish, they can score 100% on every spelling test; or second wish, they can spell all their words correctly in all their writing outside of spelling class. Which wish would students choose? Most students would choose the first wish because they have learned that it would be in their own best interest to do so. Indeed, educators have convincingly *taught* students to choose the first wish!

Instead, students must be taught that the best choice is the second wish. To help students come to this, changes need to be made. Spelling mastery must be redefined as *spelling well in writing.* Then the evaluation of spelling must focus on this achievement.

What three measures combine to form the basis for spelling evaluation in writing?

Evaluating spelling growth in writing can involve three writing formats. One format is writing produced as writing-as-a-process assignments. In a writing process assignment, writing progresses through stages of refinement to the final copy—a perfectly proofread paper. In this assignment, the student is accountable for spelling all words correctly on the final copy. The degree to which students meet this expectation is one basis for spelling evaluation.

Another format for evaluating spelling in writing is the everyday assignment that requires writing. This constitutes the majority of the writing done in a classroom. Accuracy in spelling Priority Words and any technical reference words is evaluated in this writing. The expectation is for 100% accuracy on these words. Achieving this goal should be the major factor for spelling evaluation. This baseline expectation should be met by all students who are awarded a top spelling grade. If this goal is not met, the evaluation should reflect that the most basic requirement failed to be met. Only after this basic expectation is met can a student's grade increase to the highest mark.

Another factor that should be reflected in a top spelling grade is a student's consistent ability to spell words with accuracy in everyday writing *beyond* this basic, "no-excuses" set of words. The Priority Words signify the level below which spelling literacy in a classroom will not fall.

A third format for evaluating spelling in writing is the "no-reference" write. This format is assigned two or three times during a grading period. This format differs from the everyday writing assessment in one way—no spelling references may be used. This can be a useful spelling measure when used sparingly, however it is not an authentic assessment. Adults in real-world writing are never told they cannot check an unfamiliar spelling. Part of the goal of the ***Sourcebook*** methodology is to instill in students the obligation to check an unfamiliar spelling. When this opportunity is disallowed too often, the obligation is removed. It's important to keep this obligation alive and well in the classroom.

What other factors can "count" toward the spelling grade?

Factors other than these three writing formats can be used for grading. These may include performance on the ***Sourcebook Reviews,*** the blackline master cloze activities and dictation sentences. These utilize every set of five consecutive Core Words and systematically recycle previously introduced words and skills. Teachers may also evaluate performance on the Springboard Activities in ***Sourcebooks 2, 3,*** and ***4.*** Percentages can be assigned to all these grading factors that total 100% for a final grade, but the largest percentage of the grade must be a students' ability to show competency in spelling in everyday writing, which includes having met the basic requirement of spelling Priority Words, and any technical reference words, consistently correctly.

*How does spelling evaluation based on Friday Test performance differ from evaluation based on the **Sourcebook** system?*

Yet, because the Friday Test method for evaluating spelling is familiar and convenient, some teachers may be reluctant to forgo the tests. These tests, rich with demon words, quickly and neatly spread the class across a bell-shaped curve of spelling performance. However, the scores on these tests are an invalid measure of spelling competence. They send an inaccurate and unfair message to students that spelling competence is the ability to memorize letter sequences of words for a test, regardless of how words are spelled in writing. The Friday Test provides students with their spelling grades before the goal of spelling well in writing has been reached. Again, grading and learning goals must be in alignment for effective results.

However, using the ***Sourcebook*** system for assessment, teachers and students are engaged in authentic evaluation based on spelling in *writing.* This is exactly how the community and the workplace evaluate the spelling ability of a school's graduates, and at the same time, evaluate how well the teachers in that school address spelling.

Following are general guidelines for assessing spelling competence using mastery of the Priority Words in everyday writing as a measure of growth.

What steps are necessary for using the Priority Words as the basis for spelling evaluation in writing?

1. Priority Words should be determined, and students should be made fully aware of their accountability for spelling and using the words correctly in all everyday assignments.
2. Students may use a reference list of their Priority Words as they write.
3. Teachers should give frequent writing assignments to afford students multiple opportunities to use their Priority Words across the curriculum.
4. Frequent, unannounced inspections should be made of everyday writing papers to furnish regular performance feedback toward meeting this expectation.

What data provides evaluative information on Priority Word accuracy in writing?

The writing samples that teachers use for their unannounced inspections (guideline 4) are not the only everyday writing pieces from which teachers can gather data for assessing Priority Word growth. By the time teachers have checked one classroom set of papers for Priority Words, the teachers will almost certainly have committed to memory those words on the students' Priority Word list that are often misspelled or misused. Then, as they read the dozens of other papers students produce within their writing-rich classrooms, they will find themselves automatically noting Priority Word growth on those assignments, too. Because of teachers' time constraints, the additional papers may not warrant marking the Priority Words for student performance feedback, but they do provide further evaluative information for teachers. Data for assessing spelling is thus collected mentally by teachers every time student writing is read.

Even though the Priority Word assessments cannot be quantified like the grades on a Friday Test, they are sound, professional evaluations. A comparison to some well-accepted practices in the reading arena validates this claim.

Most integrated classrooms have abandoned the old ability-grouped reading lessons with their daily read-alouds. Opportunities for independent reading have increased. Students read entire books for which their teachers hear only a small sample aloud. Yet, teachers remain competent assessors of their students' oral reading ability. Their assessments are not based on a systematic rating—in fact, few teachers ever record a grade for how their students orally read. Why? They say it's not necessary. They say they "just know" how their students are doing by checking informally, but routinely. And indeed they do know.

While students are doing less oral reading to their teachers, they are doing more writing. Every day in the integrated classroom, students write to learn . . . as they learn to write. As teachers review these multiple writing pieces, they make constant informal judgments . . . just as they do when their students read orally. And many teachers find that by informally, but routinely, noting their students' spelling of the Priority Words, they "just know" how their students are progressing—*without* a systematic record-keeping system. They simply keep a file folder of the writing samples assessed for each of their students.

How can data for Priority Word performance be monitored and transferred to a grade?

These student file folders that house the papers selected for Priority Word assessment can help teachers determine grades. Because the expectation for Priority Word performance is 100% accuracy, the file folders can be placed in two piles at the end of the grading period—those with errors, those without errors. Priority Word performance should be non-negotiable, completely objective, and be the largest factor determining the spelling grade. So, only those students who have no Priority Word errors have earned an opportunity for the top grade. If other factors that are being figured into the grade also reflect quality, the student has indeed earned a high mark. Students who fail to meet the baseline expectation for spelling, spelling their Priority Words with accuracy, have earned a much lower grade.

If teachers are setting reasonable Priority Word expectations and providing extra time for proofreading as new words are added to the list, students should make infrequent errors on these words. If frequent errors are made even among better students, this is an indicator that there are too many Priority Words. Yet, if occasional errors are made, there are various ways to record the data. Following are some options.

Teachers may record the number of Priority Word errors made in their grade book. This necessitates taking the same amount of writing for each student for each sample. With this method, progress can be noted over time. Some teachers use the Record Keeper Blackline Master (see Introduction to the Blackline Master, page 98). If this system is used, each student has a Record Keeper sheet. This may be stapled into the front of each student's Priority Word assessment file folder. Errors made are noted on this sheet, so that at the end of the grading period a record of specific errors can be summarized. Some teachers use a new Record Keeper each time an error is made and staple it to the writing piece and place it in the child's file folder. This method keeps a record of word-specific errors for each paper that has errors. The information on the Record Keeper can be recorded and kept by the teacher, by the student, or both.

How does professional judgment play a role in determining grades?

Regardless of the system used, the evaluative method must be manageable. No method should be considered that entails so much record keeping that its manageability becomes a detriment to the success of the program. For example, a system that requires Priority Word evaluations be based on scores computed on the number of words a student writes compared with the number of Priority Word errors, is unmanageable. The time it would take to administer this system is unwarranted.

Using a commonsense approach to spelling assessment, teachers simply set the specific expectation for spelling the Priority Words with accuracy. Next, they note over time how well students meet this expectation. Then, they grade according to how well students meet the goal, figuring into the grade any other factors they regard as pertinent.

Professional judgment must play a prominent role as final spelling evaluations are made. The ***Spelling Sourcebook*** methodology empowers teachers to make both instructional decisions and evaluative decisions based on their own professional judgment.

What is the main focus for evaluation in a spelling-for-writing curriculum?

The learning goal—spelling well in everyday writing—is the primary focus for spelling instruction and evaluation. To accomplish this, the Priority Words must be a priority! This priority ensures that students are not making careless spelling errors on commonly-used words, the most frustrating fault of traditional spelling programs. With the serious attention afforded these few words, proofreading in writing improves overall. Then, the spelling evaluation is based, first on meeting the basic expectation of spelling the Priority Words with accuracy. Then, if this basic goal is met, the grade is increased through performance on all other factors considered for grading.

This basic goal is so very *basic.* It *must* be an outcome for any spelling curriculum. Then, the spelling curriculum can grow in so many fine directions. One way to accommodate personal spelling growth within the spelling curriculum is through the Individualized Word List. Read on.

Article 11

Implementing the Individualized List of Words

*How is individualization incorporated in the **Spelling Sourcebook** methodology?*

The Sourcebook methodology is genuinely individualized. This is for good reason. Today's classrooms reflect more diversity than any previous time in history. So, the Spelling Sourcebook Series is designed to be customized to meet the individual needs of different school districts, schools, teachers, and students.

*How is the **Sourcebook** program individualized to a school district or school?*

First, each group of Sourcebook users is actively involved individualizing their spelling curriculum to meet their needs by using the guidelines recommended in the ***Sourcebooks.*** For example, educators divide the high-frequency words into their own grade-level sets of Core Words.

*How is the **Sourcebook** program individualized to a specific teacher?*

On the teacher level, each individual teacher chooses the Core Word Springboard Activities from the menu of options in ***Sourcebooks 2, 3,*** or ***4.*** As the teacher decides which activities to do, the difficulty of the activities is considered, as well as the skill being reinforced. The teacher also determines the format for the lessons—teacher-directed, independent, cooperative group; at school or at home. The teacher has options for testing. And the teacher determines the time frame for the instruction.

*How is the **Sourcebook** program individualized for students?*

On the student level, individualization is built into the program in several ways. As the Core Words "grow" skills, students produce many more words. Different students or student groups produce diverse word banks. For example, with the Core Word *city,* students may be asked to find and write more words that follow the same plural rule (baby/babies). Even though the word examples are individualized to each student or student group, the spelling rule being reinforced is the same.

The production of these word banks not only provides for individualization, but active cognizant involvement with the words. As words are generated, students are thinking. A *predetermined* list of words used to teach a skill would not result in this kind of enterprising student involvement.

The ***Spelling Sourcebook*** program provides three more opportunities for individualization on the student level. The Priority Words are individualized to the abilities of students and/or groups of students. When students miss Core Words and/or previously introduced Core Words on the ***Spelling Sourcebook Reviews,*** the errors provide for individualization. Teachers can identify a group of students who missed a particular word, such as substituting *its* for *it's,* and provide instruction to that group in preparation for the reoccurrence of the homophone on future Reviews. Further, each student can be expected to write a list of words that he or she missed on the Review. This list becomes an individualized list of words for study at home or at school (see Introduction to the Blackline Master, page 98).

What is the Individualized List of Words?

And finally, the ***Sourcebook*** methodology provides for the addition of an Individualized Word List for students. This extension list complements the basic program of Priority Words, Core Words, and an infinite number of Springboard Word experiences. A student's needs can be personalized with this program option. And the Individualized List is an option, not a necessity. It is recommended for implementation for all or some students once the essential aspects of the program are progressing smoothly.

Which words might an Individualized Word List include?

The words for a student's Individualized Word List can be generated by the student, by the student's parents, by the teacher. Following are suggestions for this extension list:

> the name of the street on which a student lives; the school name; the name of a student's teacher and principal; the names of a student's friends and relatives; the names of a student's pets; words pertinent to a student's hobby; the names of games, activities, clubs, or books that interest the student; words generated through activities (see Article 12, page 51).

What options are suggested for recording words for an Individualized List?

Different formats may be used for recording these words. A blackline master can be used in single-sheet form or in booklet form (see Introduction to the Blackline Master, page 98). Regular writing paper can be used, again in single-sheet form, or made into a booklet. Another method is to have students record words on a 5x7 "spelling" card.

Whatever format is chosen, the students record the words for study. Then, the teacher should check the accuracy of the spellings. It is too laborious for the teacher to assume the responsibility of listing these words.

How should the words on the Individualized List be studied?

The Individualized List of Words can be studied at home or at school. One option for study is the Independent Word-Study Procedure (see Article 6, page 27). The words can be studied independently, or students may work in pairs, with one student monitoring the other. At home, the study partner might be a parent.

How can the Individualized List be tested?

Testing any individualized list of words is difficult, if not impossible, if an authentic test is the standard. Authentic spelling testing is always within the context of a student's everyday writing. Using writing as the testing medium, the natural occurrence of a student's Individualized Words in his or her writing is often infrequent. For example, if a student lists the word *brontosaurus* on the list, but then does not routinely write about this beast, it is a challenge to authentically assess the child's ability to spell the word.

A compromise must be made. Because the words on the Individualized List only complement the basic spelling curriculum, less authentic testing can be used. A list test is suggested. A list test is not a valid test for spelling mastery because often students can spell words on a list test, particularly when the words are prestudied, yet never spell them correctly in writing. Of course, this indicates that the words were not mastered. Yet, for this one situation, for the words on the Individualized List, the words can be "tested" through a word list test.

The testing procedure can employ the same format as the Core Word preview, which is a study strategy, rather than a test (see Article 4, page 21). Yet, calling it a test will encourage students to approach it conscientiously. Students can be tested by a student or parent partner. Correctly spelled words can be marked as such on the Individualized List, while misspelled words can be identified for restudy and retesting.

How should the Individualized List be graded?

Formally grading the results of the Individualized List test is unnecessary. This is because a student's spelling grade should be determined by accomplishment within the basic program, in large part by performance on the Core Word Reviews and through assessment of the Priority Words in everyday writing.

For which students would the Individualized List be most beneficial?

The Individualized List, an extension of the basic spelling curriculum, could be especially beneficial for students who need a challenge. Two able students working as spelling partners could initiate the Individualized List in a classroom. Later, by pairing each of these students with another student new to the Individualized List, four students become participants. Then eight students, and so on.

Parents who request a spelling challenge for their child are also good candidates for the Individualized List. The individualized learning can take place at home. Then, parents can provide feedback to the teacher as to the progress the child is making. How else might the most capable students be challenged within the ***Spelling Sourcebook*** methodology? Read on.

Article 12

Creating Opportunities for Learning Beyond the Core Word List

How are the Core Words a catalyst for developing fundamental spelling and language skills?

The high-frequency Core Words are the words that provide a writer good mileage toward spelling literacy. They are the words writers use most often. Yet, the Core Words are not the total program. The Core Words might be likened to the core of an apple containing the seeds for growing a mature apple tree. The Core Words are the seeds for growing the activities that develop a full language-integrated spelling curriculum founded on a systematic progression of basic spelling skills and strategies.

Which skills do the Core Words grow?

First, the Core Word seeds grow visual skills through the Core Word preview (see Article 4, page 21). The visual ability is the dominant skill for spelling and proofreading success. During the preview procedure, students visualize a specific Core Word—a familiar word to them. They write the word from memory. Then, students check the spelling of the word against its correct spelling. As the words are checked, students practice a strategy for learning to spell and proofread *any word.* It is a process that focuses on each sequential letter in the word. Indeed, the major challenge to achieving spelling literacy is developing the ability to carefully see the individual letters in words. The preview procedure builds the skills and strategies for this.

How do the Core Words create opportunities for learning beyond the fundamental visual skills?

Following the preview, a variety of skills surface from these Core Words. More visual skills are developed, phonemic awareness is taught and practiced, students examine word patterns, word origins are analyzed, expedient spelling rules are applied, affixes are explored, writing and thinking skills unfold through experiences with exciting literature . . . an extensive menu of skill-building opportunities are taught, practiced, applied, and consistently recycled again and again for maintenance.

Where are there ready-made resources for skill growth?

Sourcebooks 2, 3, and ***4*** house the skill-building activity ideas for each Core Word 1–1200. As each high-use Core Word is introduced, the spelling curriculum grows via the selection of activities from the appropriate grade-level ***Sourcebook.*** The ***Sourcebook Reviews,*** the blackline master cloze activities and dictation sentences for each consecutive set of five Core Words, provide ongoing practice of Core Words in context. Within the ***Reviews,*** skill development is maintained through more activity options and extensive writing idea follow-ups to the activities. Then, the ***Word-Wise Sourcebooks*** provide the laugh-aloud rhymes and follow-up activities for reinforcing a variety of language skills. These creative poems all have a *purpose.* Their authors, Dr. Barbara Schmidt and Dr. Maurice Poe, weave developmentally-appropriate language learning into the rhymes and the skill-building activities that extend them.

Are teachers expected to teach all the activities?

There are far too many activities to teach them all. Instead, teachers use each of their ***Sourcebooks*** as resources from which to customize their spelling curriculum—*their way.* Teachers simply do the activities they deem appropriate, and skip the others.

How are activity selections made to ensure opportunities for a balanced learning program?

Because the ***Sourcebooks*** are designed to *complement and balance* any language and reading curriculum, teachers select those activities that best meet their global objective. For example, if teachers perceive their current reading and language program as weak in vocabulary development . . . then, vocabulary building activities can be selected for instruction from the ***Sourcebooks*** to create an overall balanced program. This selection process can be done independently by teachers, or accomplished as a group among grade-level colleagues.

How can the learning program be extended to meet the needs of students with different capabilities?

The built-in flexibility for achieving an overall balanced curriculum also provides flexibility to adjust instruction for differing learning rates and styles among students. Activities for the same word vary in difficulty. Some activities are quite sophisticated requiring original application of concepts. Thinking skills are necessary, for instance making inferences and generalizations about words and their spellings. Other activities review skills and concepts providing another exposure for initial understanding.

How can the most capable students be challenged?

The most capable students need to be challenged. One way to accomplish this is through the addition of more words to their Priority Word list. For example, if the majority of the class has a Priority Word list that includes words 1–50, then the few students for whom this would be easily accomplished can be given a Priority Word list of 1–85.

The Individualized Program helps to extend the range and number of words learned (see Article 11, page 49).

Writing is the best extension activity for spelling growth. The capable spellers, through multiple opportunities to write, generate more experiences with words. Words that are challenging to these capable students in writing can be added to their Individualized Program.

The Springboard Activities in the ***Sourcebooks*** offer another challenge to able students. Simply by increasing the expectations for selected activities, rigor is increased. For example, when a class assignment is given to find and write words with a specific spelling pattern, the able students can be asked to locate more words than the average learners. This increases their personal encounters with words and, at the same time, provides a larger bank of words for discussion among all class members.

Many of the Springboard Activities are projects and can be assigned to the most competent students. These students should present their projects orally to the class for the benefit of all students. This presentation serves as excellent readiness for students who could not have completed the activity themselves.

By increasing the performance expectations during the completion of the cloze activities and dictation sentences in the ***Sourcebook Reviews,*** abundant challenge is offered. These activities are designed to revisit the most persistently troublesome words that often burden adults. Then, these activities always engage students in follow-up exercises which also contribute to enrichment.

The ***Word-Wise Sourcebooks*** extend the program for all learners, but the competent students often garner greater insights from these laugh-aloud, language-learning rhymes and activities. The idiosyncrasies of our language are explored in this addition to the ***Sourcebooks,*** an area of interest and humor for most students of accomplished language facility.

But there are some students for whom the regular-paced curriculum is too challenging. Is it possible to meet the needs of these students using the ***Sourcebook*** approach to spelling literacy? Read on.

Helping Students With Spelling Problems

How are spelling ability and intelligence related?

Spelling and intelligence are not correlated. In fact, spelling ability is not even related to success within the language arts—speaking, listening, writing, and reading. Experience verifies this. Not all good speakers or good listeners are good spellers. Not all good writers are good spellers. Not all good readers are good spellers. However, it is rare for a good speller not to be a good reader.

What is the dominant skill for learning to spell and proofread?

Generally, good spellers have good visual skills. Certainly, the dominant modality for learning to spell English words is the visual modality. This is not true of languages with a higher sound-symbol correspondence than English, such as Spanish. Spanish words are spelled almost exactly as they sound. But what can be done to aid the poor English writer who hasn't the visual skills needed for easy access to spelling mastery?

First, it's important to note that there are no shortcuts to developing spelling skills without the use of visual skills. If a student is going to be successful in spelling and proofreading, the visual skills need to be developed. Teachers must begin on the level at which the students are currently functioning visually and build on those skills as best they can in the available time (see Article 7, page 29). This can be done in conjunction with the ideas that follow.

To help anyone with a learning problem, a key consideration is helping them believe they *can* learn. Many poor spellers are convinced they cannot spell well. Unfortunately, much of this "cannot" attitude has been taught to them through traditional spelling methodology that requires some students to miss a few words on the Friday Spelling Test. The practice of adding "challenge words" to this test ensures that only a few students are allowed to score 100% and feel successful. This teaches some students that they can spell and other students that they cannot spell . . . neither of which is true. Spelling ability cannot be determined by a test of words isolated from writing.

Some students who are experiencing difficulty with spelling may be able to be accommodated in the regular Core Word program by modifying some of the activities and providing assistance with others. This is often true for capable students who are learning English as a second language.

Why can't the Core Word list be reduced to fewer words?

In modifying the spelling unit, the list of words cannot be shortened. Because the words are taught in the order of their frequency of use in writing, skipping a few words in each unit would not be wise. However, by employing the following suggestions, the teacher can help some students be successful with the regular Core Word list.

How can independent word study be modified for students challenged by spelling?

One way of aiding poor spellers is by helping them clearly define the skills necessary for becoming a good speller—that is, the ability to slow down and carefully *see* each letter of a word while spelling and proofreading. Touching every letter of a word with a pencil point and saying its name is often helpful during spelling study and proofreading. During the independent word-study procedure (see Article 6, page 27), tracing each letter with a pencil and saying its name is a powerful study technique that can significantly aid a student challenged by learning to spell.

How can the preview be modified for students with perceptual difficulties?

For students who experience difficulty copying the spelling words from the chalkboard during the Core Word preview (see Article 4, page 21), this alternate procedure can be used. The student with perceptual problems should be seated close to the chalkboard. Next to this student should be seated a student who can capably copy the words from the board. As the capable student prints the words in the rewrite column during the self-correction procedure, he or she should softly say the name of each letter as it is written, just audibly enough for the student who has the perceptual difficulties to hear. This auditory clue provides assistance to the student who would otherwise have difficulty with this task using only the visual aid.

But the student with perceptual problems should also be asked to copy one or two words from the chalkboard using only the visual clue. The words chosen for copying must be the easiest—those that are the shortest and with the most tall and tail letters that give them a configuration that is easier to see and remember. This provides the best opportunity for these students to be successful.

Little by little over time, all auditory clues can be phased out. The visual skills are the skills that must be developed for spelling and proofreading success. As long as the auditory clues are provided, the students with perceptual problems tend to use them instead of the visual modality. While this is initially beneficial, it will eventually slow the process of developing the visual modality.

One intermediate step that could be engaged during the auditory phase-out process is supplying students with a word card on their desk to use as the model from which to copy the word into the rewrite column. This is easier than copying the word from the chalkboard. The word should be boldly printed on the word card in appropriate manuscript, or printing—not all capital letters, not cursive letters. Only one word card should be placed on the desk at a time to maximize the ability to focus attention on the word for practice.

In time, the boldly written word can be replaced with a word written on paper in regular writing size. The paper can list all the words to be presented during the preview or review correction procedure; however, only the words already corrected should be revealed to the students during the rewrite process. The words not yet corrected can be covered with a paper so that they cannot be seen.

How can activities that are too difficult for some students be made less difficult?

Core Word and Springboard Activities selected for whole-class use are very beneficial to lower-performing students, yet may be too difficult to complete without assistance. These students can frequently be accommodated by allowing them to work cooperatively with a student or students who can provide guided help.

The ***Sourcebook Reviews*** can be made less difficult. For the blackline master cloze activity, some words or the first letters of words may be filled in for students who would be challenged to do the activity in its entirety. The sentence dictation section of each ***Review*** can also be modified so that these students can experience success. A blackline master can be prepared for them, using a cloze format with the sentences to be dictated. Blanks can be substituted for selected words, or letters in words. Then, as the sentences are dictated, the students fill in only the words or letters left blank on the master.

This method allows these students to successfully participate and benefit from the dictation exercise without the frustration of being asked to hear and write each sentence in its entirety. As students gain confidence and competence with dictation, the cloze format can be adjusted to require the students to write increasingly more of the sentences being dictated.

Why is the Core Word list inappropriate for students who cannot read the words in the list?

For students with the most severe spelling problems, the Core Word list may be too difficult. These students usually have language deficits that go beyond spelling difficulties. Often, they have a reading problem. If the Core Word list cannot be easily read and understood by the students, the words are too difficult for spelling study. Words that cannot be effortlessly read are not appropriate for spelling study (see Article 3, page 17). Reading a word is far easier than spelling a word, so developmentally the reading skills must be learned for words long before the spelling skills for the same words are taught.

This is an important concept for teachers of students with language learning deficits, as well as for teachers of students for whom English is not their primary language. These students benefit from time spent on language experiences that are prerequisites to spelling development, such as hearing, speaking, and reading the language. After these students have gained facility in reading, then spelling instruction can begin. Until that time, formal spelling should not be taught.

How can language experiences be provided through the spelling curriculum for lower-performing students?

If students cannot read the Core Words, they should be excused from the Core Word preview and review. However, these students would benefit from involvement in selected Core Word and Springboard Activities with the class, particularly those activities that develop general language skills (see Article 12, page 51). Students with language deficits need an abundance of language experiences. The activities can help provide some of these experiences, as well as involve the students in learning activities with the rest of the class.

How is a proofreading reference similar to a Priority Word list?

Instead of using the regular Core Word program with these students, spelling instruction can focus on a special list of Priority Words—a list considerably shorter than the one used by the majority of the class (see Article 8, page 33, and Article 9, page 39). This special, limited list of Priority Words is best renamed so that comparisons of lists are not as easily made among students. Perhaps the terminology "proofreading reference" would work well.

The proofreading reference should consist of a limited list of words beginning with the first words on the frequency-of-use word list (see Reference 1, page 77). This targets for early mastery the words needed most often in writing. These high-use words are the most powerful, long-term words in the language and are critical for writing throughout a lifetime.

How can a proofreading reference provide an alternative program for students with spelling difficulties?

To effectively determine how many words would be appropriate for a student's proofreading reference, the first step is to study writing samples of the student. Teachers should note where the words with errors occur on the frequency-of-use list (see Reference 1, page 77). If errors occur as early as the first 10 or 12 words, this is where instruction must begin. But the student should not be insulted by having these first 12 words designated as "spelling words." Instead, give the student an alphabetized list of these words as a personal reference guide. These words are the student's proofreading reference and serve the same purpose as the Priority Word list used by other members of the class.

The words on the proofreading reference list must be spelled and proofread correctly in all writing in all classes. Students should be encouraged to use the list to check spellings. The students are *accountable* for these words. A proofreading accountability contract can be created so that students are clearly aware of this expectation.

Often, these students write very little on each written assignment. Nonetheless, they must be given many opportunities to write so that they receive repeated practice proofreading for the words on their list. The teacher should check as many papers as possible, as often as possible, for these words. All teachers who work with these students need to make a cooperative effort to do the same thing. Aggressive emphasis must be placed on learning to spell and proofread these high-use words.

For the time, other misspelled words on the papers of these students can be ignored. Only so many words can be a priority at one time. The highest-frequency words are a higher priority than other words. When the students have gained facility spelling and proofreading these words, they will have developed a bank of words that will serve them in their writing forever.

How is a Core Word list developed for students for whom the regular Core Word list is too difficult? How should the words be studied?

While reviewing students' papers, the teacher will find that many of the proofreading reference words are spelled correctly. These correct spellings should be acknowledged and the students' proofreading efforts complimented. The proofreading reference words that are misspelled or misused then become the words for study. These words are the students' Core Words.

Students can study these words using a variety of methods. For the homophones, context sentences for reference can be provided. For misspellings, activities can include use of the independent word-study procedure, finding words within the words, creating mnemonic devices for remembering the spelling of the words, tracing the letters of the words on sandpaper to kinesthetically feel the letters being made. In addition, visual perception and discrimination activities are recommended (see Article 7, page 29). It is the visual modality that must be strengthened before significant, long-term spelling and proofreading progress can be achieved.

How should students correct spelling errors?

When the writing pieces are returned to the students for corrections of errors for the words on their proofreading reference, it's beneficial to have the students erase the entire word and rewrite it, rather than fix only the letters that need changing. Students should follow the same procedure when proofreading written work prior to handing it in. This provides practice writing the word as a total left-to-right process.

As the students show progress in spelling and proofreading the words on their proofreading reference list, the next step is to add a few more words for which the students must assume accountability. Just as with the Priority Words, the next words added are those on the frequency-of-use word list that follow the last word on the proofreading reference. The new spelling reference list should be realphabetized. Then students and teachers can proceed as before.

How will the proofreading reference program promote spelling progress in writing?

Students with severe spelling problems can be taught to spell. But because these students learn to spell more slowly than others and may never learn to spell as large a bank of words from memory, it's important to use spelling time efficiently. By developing visual skills and focusing instruction on words at the beginning of the frequency-of-use list, visible spelling progress in writing can be made. Simultaneously, this progress generates feelings of success that, in turn, motivates students to learn.

For these students, mastery in writing of the highest-frequency writing words can clearly be identified as *major* progress. Focusing on these words is the most time-efficient and effort-efficient way to help the students develop visible evidence that they are becoming better spellers in their writing. It pinpoints instruction precisely on those words that are the most necessary for everyday writing.

But are students really learning to spell these words if they always use a spelling reference? Students should be not only allowed, but required to use spelling references. It is important to promote their use. Students must learn that it is acceptable to use spelling references and totally unacceptable *not* to use them when there is doubt about the spelling of a word for which they have been made accountable. Because most of the words for which the students are initially being made accountable are used in almost every writing piece, the words eventually become committed to memory from their continual use.

How can dictation reinforce selected words for study on the proofreading reference list?

For more reinforcement of the proofreading reference words, teachers can create a cloze-format dictation activity (as previously described on pages 54–55) in which students fill in the missing words or letters of words without using their reference lists. This activity allows the teacher and students to note which words are still overly challenging and which are well on their way to mastery.

This cloze activity can be modified to be used as an independent exercise rather than as dictation. The students read the cloze sentences silently, using context clues to figure out the missing words. If more than one word would make sense in a blank, one or two letters could be provided to limit the possibilities.

What is the best way to help students challenged by spelling?

Constant reinforcement, encouragement, and verification of progress are important for students who are challenged by spelling. It should be made clear to them that spelling is a skill that challenges many bright people. The most practical approach for teaching these students is to focus on helping them master as large a bank of high-use words as possible and cultivate in them the habit of using spelling references to assist them for the spellings of words outside the bank.

As special programs are designed and implemented for students with spelling problems, the students' parents should be informed about the program. Most parents will be interested in knowing the spelling goals that have been specially set for their child and how they might help their child to achieve these goals.

Working with parents is a significant part of any successful curriculum, no matter what the ability level of the students. How can all parents be informed of and included in the spelling challenges and progress of their child? Read on.

Article 14

Informing and Involving Parents

All parents want their children to be academically successful, and most parents are willing to help their children toward this goal. Spelling is one area in which they are usually comfortable offering help. Over the years, parents have learned that most teachers send home a weekly spelling list to be tested on Friday. And mastery has traditionally been defined as the ability to spell the words correctly on the Friday Test.

How does traditional spelling mastery differ from ***Spelling Sourcebook*** *mastery?*

One of the differences between a traditional spelling program and the ***Spelling Sourcebook*** methodology is the change in the definition of spelling mastery. Mastery of the spelling words is no longer based on a once-a-week test of words in isolation. Instead, students must spell words correctly *every day* in their writing. All words must be spelled correctly on the final copy of writing pieces that have developed through the writing process. On all everyday assignments, selected words must be spelled correctly (see Article 8, page 33, and Article 9, page 39). So spelling mastery is achieved in writing, not on a test of isolated words apart from purposeful writing.

What results do parents want from spelling instruction?

Parents want their children to spell words correctly in writing. They want to see genuine evidence in their children's school assignments and at-home writing (such as telephone messages and letters to the grandparents) that spelling has been taught and learned. Parents are often uncomfortable when they see misspellings in student writing. Indeed, the increased emphasis on spelling mastery in writing will receive enthusiastic support from parents.

What key concepts should be shared with parents?

This support develops as a result of understanding the new program. The ***Spelling Sourcebook*** methodology needs to be thoroughly shared with parents prior to its implementation. Information presented to the parents should compare the old and new methodology and cite examples of the benefits that can be expected to result from use of the new program. As teachers describe the features of the new program, it is important to tie each feature directly to a desired benefit. Following are key features of the ***Spelling Sourcebook*** program with anticipated benefits.

1. Emphasis on Life Skills

1. Increased parent and teacher dissatisfaction with students' spelling in writing was the catalyst for making a change in the spelling curriculum. The new program is aligned with life skills emphasizing spelling in everyday writing.

   Benefit: Students learn to spell words where spelling really counts . . . in their everyday writing. In real life, people need to know how to spell in writing, not just on a spelling test. Employers do not give spelling tests on Fridays, but expect that job applicants and employees produce error-free spelling in their written communications. Your child will be better prepared to meet this challenge using the new program.

2. High-Frequency Writing Words

2. The new program emphasizes absolute mastery in writing of the most commonly-used writing words, but provides word experiences with hundreds of additional words for spelling and language growth.

   Benefit: Students spend their spelling time mastering the words that are used most often in writing, not memorizing the letter sequences of seldom-used words, only to forget the spellings after the test. Your child will be taught to spell precisely those words a writer needs throughout a lifetime of everyday writing.

3. Early Spelling Success

3. Spelling and writing are tightly bonded. This bonding is achieved through the high-use writing words, as well as the way they are presented. The high-utility words are introduced through the grade levels in the order of their frequency of use in writing. For example, *the* is the highest-frequency word in our language, so it is the first word taught. The second most frequently-used word *of,* is introduced next, and so on.

   Benefit: Even beginning writers will be able to spell many words correctly in their writing, regardless of the writing topic. This early spelling success in writing will make young writers feel good about themselves and will encourage them to write and spell with more confidence. The new program will introduce your first grader to spelling that will form the foundation for spelling well in writing throughout the grades.

4. Adaptability

4. Teachers using the ***Spelling Sourcebook*** methodology take responsibility for making the same kinds of decisions for teaching spelling that they are accustomed to making in all other curriculum areas. For example, teachers decide on which day to begin a spelling unit, how many words are appropriate for the unit, what activities to select for teaching and extending the unit, and when to conclude the unit. With a traditional program, these decisions were predetermined by the program.

   Benefit: Teachers can adapt their spelling instruction to better serve the needs and interests of your child, as well as other students in the class. Your child's spelling achievement should increase with a program that can easily be adapted to the students and the classroom climate.

5. Research-based Methods

5. The results of years of research in spelling acquisition are incorporated into the new program. This research includes use of a self-corrected pretest (the Core Word preview). All teachers use this procedure to initiate word study. The research-supported independent word-study procedure is also a staple in the program.

   Benefit: Because your child is learning to spell through tried-and-tested methods, your child will learn to spell with greater ease in less time.

6. Related Language Learning

6. The commonly-used writing words are not the total program, only its nucleus. Multiple motivational activities extend spelling study to hundreds of additional words. These activities provide opportunities for learning that include spelling rules, phonics for spelling, word patterns (*bright, sight, light*), word prefixes and suffixes, and many additional related language skills. Prominent among the extension activities is writing. Teachers are provided with ready-made resources for including these activities in their classroom.

   Benefit: Students are introduced to such a variety of activities that they'll find spelling and its relationship with other language skills exciting. Through these many activities, teachers have the resources to build on the basic program in a way that will best meet the learning needs of your child.

7. Review-oriented Program

7. The new program is designed so that the words and the basic skills in the program are continuously reviewed. The traditional workbook programs introduced words, they were tested on Friday, and then the words vanished. A specific skill was the focus of one unit—then, dismissed. Now words and skills are revisited again and again.

   Benefit: There is a long-term mastery, rather than short-term learning, of words and skills for your child.

8. Spelling in Writing

8. Spelling evaluation is aligned with the spelling goal—a student's ability to spell and proofread words in writing, not on a test apart from writing. Students are accountable for spelling a select group of the highest-use words, their Priority Words, correctly in all writing. Random, regular checks of assignments for spelling accuracy of these words is the major determiner of spelling performance. A reference is provided for these words. But performance in no-reference writing assignments and in writing-as-a-process assignments that require error-free final copies also measure spelling skills.

   Benefit: Your child will better understand and attain the spelling goal when spelling in writing determines the spelling grade.

9. A Child-specific Approach

9. Students can maintain an Individualized List of spelling words. This list consists of word errors in everyday writing and may also include words selected by the students, words generated through the extension activities, and other words pertinent to student writing selected by parents and teachers.

   Benefit: Your child's specific spelling needs and interests can be accommodated through the Individualized List.

10. Cost Efficiency

10. The old spelling books that used traditional word lists and lessons were not only a recurring expense, but their use did not ensure that students would be capable of spelling well outside of spelling class in their everyday writing. Student spelling books are not used in the new program. Students practice spelling through the writing they do all day long, every day, for every subject, for every teacher. Further, spelling skills and concepts are routinely selected for instruction from an abundant menu of activity options in teacher resource books that support the program.

    Benefit: School funds can be better spent, and your child's time and effort in learning to spell will be more effective through the ***Spelling Sourcebook*** methodology used in the new program.

11. Parent Participation at Home

11. Parents can help at home by developing spelling accountability in writing and by assisting with activities that develop the basic spelling skills. When teachers send home everyday writing pieces that were earmarked for parent-child review of the Priority Words, parents can set aside time to proofread these papers with their child. If spelling errors among the Priority Words are found, parents can guide their child through the independent word-study procedure. Homophone errors can be discussed, using context sentences for the homophones as models for usage. Further, when students are asked to do skill-development assignments from the ***Sourcebooks*** or the ***Reviews*** as homework, parents can assist them.

    Benefit: You can contribute to your child's spelling growth by helping your child learn to be his or her own personal editor for writing pieces, as well as help toward the acquisition of basic spelling skills in your child's skill-based homework.

12. Parent Participation at School

12. Parents can also assist the teacher by helping to check spelling in writing at school. They can check the spellings of Priority Words in everyday school assignments. They can check spellings in no-reference writing assignments and help students progress toward error-free papers in writing-as-a-process assignments.

    Benefit: You can contribute to your child's spelling growth at school, as well as to the growth in spelling literacy of other students.

Parents should be encouraged to discuss their child's spelling curriculum with the teacher and to ask questions. They can be invited to observe the teaching of spelling in the classroom. A copy of their child's Priority Words should be provided, as well as information on the independent word-study procedure (see Article 6, page 27). Parents can be shown how to use context sentences to help their child learn the correct usage of Priority Word homophones. A bibliography of the research could be made available to interested parents (see Reference 6, page 95).

Following is an example of a letter that can be used to introduce the ***Spelling Sourcebook*** methodology to parents. The letter should be modified to meet the needs of particular teachers and parents.

What should an introductory letter to parents include?

Dear Parents,

We're introducing a new spelling program to your child. It emphasizes correct spelling in writing—a goal we know you support. Yes, now we have a plan for changing "invented spelling" to "real spelling" in your child's writing!

Here's how it works. Attached is a brief list of the words research says are used most often in writing. The highlighted words are the words your child can *never misspell or misuse* . . . in any writing, for any teacher, any day of the week. The list will grow over time, but words are never removed. Special words will be added to the list for a brief time as your child writes on a particular topic. Your child must meet an even higher spelling standard for "writing process" papers which, like before, must be letter perfect for *every word.*

We want these words on the list to be taken seriously every time your child writes. We'll choose random assignments from your child to see how well the expectation is being met. It follows then, that the spelling grade will show how well your child meets this goal.

This change was made so that your child will know that spelling "counts" in writing, exactly the way it does in the "real world." No longer will there be a Friday Test of words that your child memorized the night before *just for the test.* Now there's a test *every day* as your child writes in all the subjects. This will give your child more spelling practice than ever before. It will make sure the important words are really learned *forever,* not just for Friday.

Basic skills are a part of spelling here at Oak School. The teachers have ready-made activities in their teacher guides for teaching the well-researched spelling strategies and all the skills—phonics, spelling rules, patterns, word origins, etc. As these skills are taught and practiced, the important words are reviewed again and again. Activities also introduce hundreds of additional words to your child.

You're invited to come to school to see a short video about this new program. Choose one of the showings listed below. In the meantime, ask your child for the papers we'll be sending home to check for spelling. Work together to help your child learn to be his or her own personal spelling editor. Also, ask your child to tell you what the spelling homework assignment is for the night.

Every child can learn to spell where it really counts—in everyday writing!

*Is there a video to introduce the **Sourcebook** methodology to parents?*

In addition to this letter, the Introduction to Parents Video (40 minutes available from Northwest Textbook) will help parents feel comfortable. Then parents must be kept informed of the progress being made. How can this progress be determined, measured, and communicated on a long-range basis? Read on.

Evaluating the Spelling Curriculum

Evaluating the spelling curriculum encompasses many factors, foremost among them is student performance. Learning is the schools' product. How can a student's progress in learning to spell be measured? It can be done on a short-term and a long-term basis.

Spelling performance evaluation, short-term or long-term, must be founded on students' ability to spell in writing . . . not on a list test of the words in isolation, not on dictated sentences, not on a letter fill-in test, not on a proofreading test. *Authentic* evaluation is always tied to the learning goal. And, the learning goal for spelling is spelling well *in writing.*

How can short-term, ongoing spelling evaluation of students be achieved?

Short-term, ongoing spelling evaluation for student grades can be achieved through six kinds of assessments. First, and most important, is the random weekly selection of everyday writing papers to determine the spelling accuracy of the Priority Words. Spelling this brief list of basic, high-use words consistently correctly in everyday writing is *essential* and represents the level below which spelling literacy must not fall. Spelling performance on writing-as-a-process papers is another grading option. Third, a no-reference write can be assigned a few times each grading period to determine spelling ability *without* the use of a reference. Fourth, student effort and accuracy on assigned Springboard Activities can contribute a portion of the grade. Finally, performance on the ***Sourcebook Reviews,*** the blackline master cloze activities and dictation sentences for every consecutive set of five Core Words can supply two additional forms of information for the final grade. These sources provide ample data for grading (see Article 10, page 45).

Long-term spelling evaluation is often attempted through standardized testing, normed so that comparisons can be made. But standardized tests are not an authentic spelling evaluation, so the comparisons made from them are also invalid. Caution must be exercised regarding standardized spelling tests and the resulting scores.

What do standardized spelling tests measure?

Standardized tests do not measure how well students can spell when they write. They are proofreading tests, but it is questionable whether they even measure proofreading ability. All that can be said with confidence is that standardized spelling tests measure the ability to take standardized spelling tests. Unfortunately, this ability does not have much practical application outside a school testing environment.

How does the format of a standardized spelling test contribute to invalid scores?

Various proofreading formats are used on these tests, such as choosing the correct spelling of a word from four choices. Some students may have little difficulty correctly spelling or proofreading for these words in their own writing, but be unable to identify the correct spellings in an unfamiliar proofreading test format. These students would score low on a standardized spelling test, but have achieved considerable facility to spell well in writing. Because the proofreading format of the test engages different thought processes than are used in actual spelling in writing, the test score would report invalid information regarding spelling ability for these students.

How does the content of a standardized spelling test contribute to invalid scores?

The problems of standardized spelling testing go beyond the format of the tests. The content of the tests should also be questioned. Schools are rapidly becoming discouraged with traditional spelling methodology that focuses on long lists of seldom-used words. They are searching for options to align spelling with writing and focus on high-utility writing words. Yet, some of the words that appear on standardized spelling tests are the tricky "demon" words that are used infrequently in writing. It is unfortunate that few testmakers have changed the content of their tests to align with the changes that are occurring in the spelling curriculum. However, given the testmakers' sales volumes for these tests, it is easy to understand why they conclude that they are publishing a desirable product that is in no need of revision.

Why are standardized spelling tests used?

Using standardized spelling test scores to assess spelling competence is unfair to students, parents, and educators. Why, then, are the tests so widely used? Why, then, is so much emphasis placed on their results? One reason is that standardized spelling tests are traditional testing devices. For decades, the scores have been relied on to screen students for certain educational programs. Even when educators recognize the severe limitations of the tests and the inappropriate interpretation of the resulting data, the system perpetuates their use.

Now forward-thinking educators are beginning to rethink this issue. These leaders understand the need for spelling expectations *in writing* with routine inspections to determine student performance. They are paving the way for changes that are long overdue.

What skills are essential to standardized spelling-test performance?

However, until the changes are made students can be guided to perform better on these tests. The ***Sourcebook*** methodology teaches, practices, and evaluates the skills that increase students' ability to score well on all traditional standardized spelling tests. These tests are all proofreading tests and the ***Sourcebook*** methods for acquiring proofreading skills extensively surpass any other spelling approach. Students are taught how to proofread, they practice proofreading every day, and they're graded on their ability to proofread. This emphasis on proofreading serves students well for spelling in writing, as well as for taking standardized spelling tests. Students engaged in this comprehensive proofreading are indeed improving their standardized spelling test scores.

Further, students learn "spelling logic" through the ***Sourcebook*** activities. For instance, students learn spelling rules that can be applied to hundreds of words. They learn about spelling regularities and irregularities. For example, they learn that the *oi*, rather than the *oy*, spelling option is used far more often in the middle of a word. But the *oy* is used exclusively at the end of a word. This helps students "best guess" spellings for unfamiliar words on a standardized spelling test.

What benefit can be anticipated from teaching the format of the test?

Another factor that improves standardized spelling-test scores is teaching the format of the test. Instruction and practice with the exact format of the test can be provided just prior to administering the test. This practice should not include any of the words that are on the actual test, or criticism could be leveled for "teaching to the test."

Is there a valid substitute for standardized spelling tests? Writing samples are the best measure of spelling performance—written with or without a spelling reference. Following is a plan using the no-reference write.

What is a valid measure of spelling proficiency?

> At the beginning of the school year, and four to six times throughout the school year, teachers can assign a no-reference write to students on a given or student-selected topic.

Students should proofread their writing without access to any spelling or homophone-usage aids. Each student's misspellings of high-use words within a predetermined bank, such as misspellings among the first 100 words on the frequency-of-use list (see Reference 1, page 77), can be recorded. This data can be used to note the following:

- individual student progress over time
- comparisons among classes of the same grade level within a school
- comparisons among different grades within a school
- comparisons of the same grade among different schools in a school district
- comparisons of different grades among different schools in a school district
- comparisons among students in different schools in different cities, states, or regions

The progress can be summarized and graphically charted. For example, a graph might show a third-grade class progressing from the initial no-reference write with results indicating no errors for the first 27 words to the second no-reference write revealing no errors through word 36. This emphasizes success and clearly creates a progressive goal structure that makes student achievement exciting to educators. It focuses attention on authentic results in writing, with the writing papers to substantiate the progress.

How should homophone errors be reported?

This plan can be modified in many ways, yet still evaluate and validate "spelling for writing" instruction. For example, spelling and usage errors may be reported separately. Misuse of high-frequency homophones is a persistent problem in every-day writing. Their misuse is often so abundant that it lowers the overall evaluative results. However, the homophone errors must be reported in some form as they represent an incorrect choice of letters for the desired word. Their mastery is essential to spelling and writing success.

But it may be argued that grouping homophone errors and regular misspellings together in the evaluative summaries places a very desirable priority on instruction and mastery of the homophones that cannot be duplicated if the errors are reported independently. If teachers know that students' spelling scores on their no-reference writes reflect the use of common homophones, they may provide more practice of these homophones in daily lessons. This is a clear example of testing that determines teaching. And perhaps it is to the student writers' ultimate advantage to be the recipient of this condition.

Why does the evaluation of writing include spelling assessment?

As changes in the spelling curriculum are made that closely align spelling with writing, alternatives to standardized spelling testing need to be implemented to mirror these changes. Immense progress has been made scoring writing samples to reflect a writer's actual ability to communicate ideas through written words. And progress is also being made in including the spelling of the high-frequency words in this evaluation. Because standards for workplace literacy dictate that even the finest written ideas are unacceptable if they are not communicated through conventional English spellings, writing evaluation is now striving to encompass spelling literacy.

Through enlightened spelling and writing evaluations, alternatives to standardized testing are beginning to provide *meaningful* data. Further, good evaluative alternatives can take the focus off of the standardized spelling-test results, leading the way for their demise.

What positive outcome is emerging from standardized spelling-test data?

But some good has indeed come from the standardized spelling tests. The disappointing scores on these tests often provide a catalyst within a school district to examine the spelling curriculum. Though the initial intent of this examination is to improve the negative test scores, the whole issue of spelling instruction is showcased. Alas, the proof that students cannot spell is found not in the standardized spelling-test scores, but through the misspellings that proliferate within their writing!

Astute educators discover that the spelling solution does not lie in improving the low standardized spelling-test scores. They know that increased energy expended to teach spelling for the purpose of increasing the test scores would be a disservice to education. But what is the solution?

The solution is to improve students' spelling in writing and then to use their writing as the basis for spelling evaluation. This can be achieved through the ***Spelling Sourcebook*** methodology, which integrates spelling meaningfully throughout language learning and clearly holds students increasingly accountable for their spellings as they develop as writers. It is critical that the focus for spelling be placed squarely on performance in *everyday writing* and that all instruction and evaluation support that effort. As this approach gains acceptance, standardized spelling tests will lose their assumed pertinency.

What factors, besides student performance, should be considered during evaluation?

But for curriculum evaluation to be thorough, it needs to consider other factors beyond student achievement. For example, attitudes about spelling need to be measured. How do teachers, students, administrators, and parents feel about the spelling curriculum? Often, increased achievement generates motivation and positive attitudes. Likewise, motivation and positive attitudes generate increased achievement. It is difficult to know which comes first, as they are partners in success.

In addition to student progress and overall attitudes, spelling curriculum evaluation may also examine other factors. These may include factors such as instructional time spent on spelling, costs to implement and maintain the curriculum, management of the program, and benefits to the development of related language skills. Each of these factors can be considered to evaluate the degree to which a spelling curriculum has been successful. But the most convincing factor for success of a spelling curriculum is whether or not students have become responsible spellers in their everyday writing.

How does assessment affect instruction?

Responsible spelling in writing *can* be achieved and ability *can* be measured. One last word—the way in which spelling ability is measured determines the focus for instruction. If singular value is placed on producing high standardized spelling-test scores, the instructional program will focus on this achievement. This, then, becomes the learning goal. If this singular focus is perceived to be the most honorable, then language-integrated spelling instruction geared toward spelling well in writing will not best serve that goal. If, on the other hand, spelling in writing *is* the goal . . . read on. When should spelling instruction begin?

Article 16

Deciding When Spelling Instruction Should Begin

Young students come to first grade eager to learn to read and write. They believe they *will* learn to read and write! None of them think they'll experience difficulty developing the skills necessary to do these tasks. All first graders are very motivated to learn!

How does skill instruction in literature-based reading differ from skill instruction in traditional basal approaches?

The literature-based reading methodology builds on this motivation during the first school experience. In first grade, teachers, using predictable story structures and familiar songs and rhymes, introduce their students to "reading." That is, the students *think* they're reading; they're *saying* the boldly written words displayed before them on charts or in Big Books. But once the students think they're reading, they're feeling successful—good about themselves, school, and books. They eagerly anticipate each new day with enthusiasm fostered from their previous successes and the pleasures of literature.

All the traditional skills are meaningfully taught, practiced, and applied within a conscientious literature-based reading and language curriculum. The literature forms the base from which all the skills systematically unfold. The literature and the methodical skill instruction form a partnership that provides the "seeds" for developing the skills. Over time, competence develops.

Students are now reading sooner. Likewise, the students are writing sooner and writing more. Often the literature they read and hear is the catalyst for their writing. The young authors ardently imitate the story structures of the literature—and bloom as writers themselves. That is, the students *think* they're writing. But their writing pieces are laced with mechanical errors and misspellings. These young authors do not enter school with banks of words they can spell and use with precision. However, this lack of written language facility rarely slows their enthusiasm if they are learning in a supportive environment that encourages every attempt at language use. And that's the way it should be.

Why are language approximations appropriate for early learners?

These early experiences with reading and writing parallel the development of learning to talk. Babies begin by imitating sounds that eventually make words. Their first attempts at speaking are only approximations of "real talk," but with encouragement and repeated practice, coherent and meaningful speech develops. If children were expected to speak with immediate competence and reprimanded if they didn't, little progress would be made learning to talk.

This is equally true for reading and writing. Just as early learners approximate speaking to learn to speak, they approximate reading to learn to read, and they approximate writing to learn to write. The approximations are natural, acceptable steps toward becoming competent language users.

Spelling skills develop in a predictable fashion through writing. Young writers begin writing letter-like shapes strung loosely together. When they become aware that letters make sounds, then their writing reflects letters that make the sounds in the words they're attempting to write. The first sound-to-letter connections are made with consonants. Vowels appear in students' spellings later. With time, the young writers begin writing actual words, or letter combinations that approximate real words.

Why is "temporary spelling" better terminology than "invented spelling"?

The letter sequences used to approximate conventional spellings are often referred to as "invented spellings." However, they might be termed "temporary spellings" to help young students better understand the transition the words should undergo as their writing develops and they fine-tune their spelling skills.

What are spelling readiness skills?

When, then, should spelling instruction begin? In a sense, spelling instruction begins long before it is given the label "spelling instruction." Readiness for formal spelling instruction includes learning letters of the alphabet, holding a pencil, using left-to-right orientation, learning that talk can be written and writing can be read, and understanding that the letters that comprise words often stand for sounds.

When should spelling instruction begin?

Once these skills and concepts are mastered and the students have developed a bank of words they are comfortable reading, actual spelling instruction can begin. This usually takes place the second half of first grade. At this time, most students can read the words that they will be asked to learn to spell. And all students must be able to read their spelling words . . . with ease. It is from the bank of reading words that spelling words are chosen (see Article 3, page 17).

Two or three Core Words can be introduced at a time. First, the Core Words are used as "seeds" to grow visual skills on the preview. Then the teacher can "springboard" from the Core Words to many developmentally appropriate skill-building activity options listed in ***Sourcebook 2***. In these activities, students gain exposure to many more words. A few of the first Core Words serve as Priority Words to develop spelling accountability (see Article 8, page 33, and Article 9, page 39).

What is the teaching process for beginning spelling instruction?

The important words and skills are reinforced again and again through the ***Sourcebook Reviews***. After every set of five Core Words has been presented on a preview (probably on two separate previews) and developed through the Springboard Activities, a ***Review*** can be given. These are the blackline master cloze activities and dictation sentences with activity follow-ups. Teachers can ease their students into a successful experience with the ***Reviews*** by following the teaching suggestions in the ***Reviews*** preface.

Which words are appropriate for introduction to beginning writers?

Knowing how to spell just the first eight words on the frequency-of-use list provides a sound foundation for spelling in writing. In fact, these eight words (*the, of, and, a, to, in, is, you*) constitute 18% of the words student and adult writers use in their everyday writing (see Article 2, page 9). Beginning writers reflect a higher use of the word *I* (word 24 in frequency) and a somewhat lower use of the word *of.* However, the probability that the beginning writer's writing will contain the highest use words on a frequency-of-use list is great. These high-use words provide beginning writers with the look of emerging literacy in their writing, as well as form the foundation for spelling throughout a lifetime.

What problems can be anticipated if spelling experiences are deferred until later?

If attention to spelling these high-use words is deferred until second or third grade, as many experts feel is preferable, the young writers may have already written the words incorrectly hundreds of times. This only serves to reinforce—over and over again—the incorrect spellings. Teachers in subsequent grades then find that what were initially labeled temporary spellings have become nearly permanent. Further, the students are no longer motivated to learn the spellings of these "baby words." Teachers have been praising the students' writing for years without much attention drawn to these misspellings, so it is understandable that the students do not feel the need to change.

Indeed, it is wise to take full advantage of the enthusiasm first graders share for learning to spell in their writing. Spelling can be a positive and rewarding experience for beginning writers. It can be integrated into the development of other language skills and approached in a considerably less structured way than the spelling instruction that follows in subsequent grades. It can be fun! First grade is the most teachable moment for introducing and mastering a few of the high-use writing words that are critical to spelling literacy. The words can form the foundation for spelling in writing.

Why should a formal program of multiple spelling words be avoided in grade one?

How many words in all should be introduced to first graders? That decision is for first-grade teachers to make. But "covering" many words should not be the goal. Teachers should focus on developing the concept that words have correct spellings and that writers spell correctly in order to make it easier for readers to understand their writing. At the first-grade level, introducing a few words in a variety of language-related activities is better than presenting many words and focusing strictly on spelling. The spelling words should serve as a catalyst for learning other language skills.

How can a few Core Words become a catalyst for developing related language skills?

Therefore, the few Core Words introduced in first grade form a base from which to refine spelling skills in subsequent grades, as well as providing a vehicle for building language facility. The language experiences unfold from the limited number of Core Words through extension activities. These activities introduce many more words for exposure and discussion, so that students can make generalizations about words and their spellings. Students learn to be discriminating observers of words through multiple experiences with them. In addition to expanding the first-grade word bank, the extension activities offer opportunities for developing listening, reading, speaking, and writing skills.

These extension activities can take many forms. For example, rhyming patterns can be created using the high-frequency Core Words *and, that, it, on.* The patterns can serve as a word bank for writing rhymes. The rhymes can be printed on large charts to be read by students in choral groups—rhyme, rhythm, repetition! The students can then write their favorite rhymes, illustrate them, and compile them into a class book to be read and listened to by all.

What resources are available for teaching and extending the Core Words?

One resource for these ideas that teach and extend the Core Words is included in the ***Spelling Sourcebook*** Series, not only for first grade, but for words through frequency 1200. Teachers need not create the ideas and activities on their own, but simply select from a menu of options housed in ***Spelling Sourcebooks 2, 3,*** and ***4.***

Further, the ***Sourcebook Reviews*** provide ongoing reinforcement of the Core Words and skills so that students receive sufficient exposure and practice for long-term learning. The ***Reviews*** are blackline master cloze activities and dictation sentences for every set of five high-frequency Core Words. Many of the cloze activities at the early levels focus on well-known literature books to complement the literature-based curriculum. First grade teachers should use the ***Reviews*** for High-Use Writing Words 1–400. These ***Reviews*** correlate with ***Sourcebook 2***.

The ***Word-Wise Sourcebooks*** are exciting laugh-aloud rhymes for learning language skills. Level 1 is appropriate for first graders. This addition to the program abounds with developmentally appropriate activities, each initiated by a blackline master rhyme that helps young learners become "word-wise." Teachers can extend their entire language program through the use of the rhymes and activities for use at school and at home.

The philosophy for implementing the ***Spelling Sourcebook*** methodology has been addressed throughout the previous Articles of this book. Now, how do teachers actually get started teaching their grade using this methodology? For specific guidelines on getting started, read on.

Article 17

Teaching the Program: How to Get Started

What prerequisite is there to a successful implementation of the ***Sourcebook*** *methodology?*

Each of the Articles 1–16 of ***Spelling Sourcebook 1,*** the Program Description, needs to have been read and reflected upon before Article 17 is considered. A prerequisite to a successful implementation of the ***Spelling Sourcebook*** methodology is a thorough understanding of it. If teachers attempt to teach the program using the old, traditional spelling principles, the results will be disappointing. The new methodology is carefully explained within Articles 1–16.

What are the two outcomes, or goals, of the ***Sourcebook*** *program?*

The description of the program heretofore outlines a total spelling program that has two major purposes. One major goal is to develop "spelling logic," or an overall understanding of spelling and proofreading skills and concepts. This includes a knowledge of sound-letter awareness, or phonics. It includes a facility with spelling patterns, usable spelling rules, word origins, affixes, visual perception for spelling and proofreading accuracy, homophone usage . . . and dozens of language-related skills, such as vocabulary development. This part of the program is developed through ongoing activities provided in ***Spelling Sourcebooks 2, 3,*** and ***4*** with the Core Words and Springboard Words and Activities.

The foremost goal of the ***Spelling Sourcebook*** methodology is to ensure that student writing reflects a look of literacy regarding spelling. This is basic to any spelling program. This is the single, most important outcome of spelling instruction and is achieved through a careful commitment to developing accountability for spelling as students' writing skills mature. This part of the ***Spelling Sourcebook*** methodology is cultivated mainly through the Priority Words and practiced within students' everyday writing across the curriculum.

What is the first step for achieving the goal of learning spelling and proofreading skills and concepts?

To get started, teachers need their Core Word list for their grade level. The Core Words are the words that develop spelling and related skills and concepts. Your Core Word list was developed from the ***Spelling Sourcebook 1*** word bank (see Reference 1, page 77) that lists and numbers words in their order of frequency of use in student and adult writing. The Core Word list divided by grade level reflects a customized set of words—customized by the educators with which this specific program will be used. These educators predetermined which words from the word bank will be introduced at each grade level. Assignment of the words by grade level is recorded on page 11. These words, then are a teacher's Core Words from which the skill and concept growth in the program unfold. These Core Words are not the program, but the "seeds" for growing a sense of spelling logic that develops over time within the program.

How is a skill-building unit introduced?

The introduction of the Core Words for each unit begins this "growth" through instruction and practice of a strategy that builds visual skills for learning to spell and proofread any word. This process is called the Core Word preview (see Article 4, page 21). Teachers can select the first few words in order on their list for the preview. Teachers should think of the preview as a *strategy* that is taught and practiced through the Core Words, but pertains to lifetime spelling and proofreading accuracy. It is not a test.

What skill is developed through independent word study?

For some or all students, the independent word-study procedure (see Article 6, page 27) can follow the preview. This procedure, like the preview, is a strategy-building activity that helps students carefully see each letter in a word sequentially. Perhaps the biggest challenge to spelling and proofreading facility is developing the ability to see a word and its separate letter parts. Both the preview and the independent word-study procedure do this. The main difference between the two lies in their administration. The preview is teacher directed, while the independent word study is learner directed.

How is skill and concept instruction expanded?

Following the visual skill-building activities, perhaps the next day, the teacher selects activities to expand the program to multiple spelling and language-related skills and concepts, to experiences with dozens and dozens of additional words beyond the Core Words for that unit, and to activities that review Core Words and skills. The activities are selected from ***Spelling Sourcebooks 2, 3,*** and ***4.*** Following are guidelines for using these books:

Sourcebook 2 Activities for Core Words 1–400 (grades 1–4)

Sourcebook 3 Activities for Core Words 401–800 (grades 5–6)

Sourcebook 4 Activities for Core Words 801–1200 (grades 7 and above)

What Sourcebook materials do teachers need?

To teach the program, all teachers need a personal copy of this book, ***Spelling Sourcebook 1***. All teachers need the ***Sourcebook*** that houses their Core Word activity options, either ***Sourcebook 2, 3,*** or ***4.*** Further, teachers must have their own copy of ***Sourcebook Reviews*** that correspond to their Core Words. The ***Reviews*** are the source for the blackline master cloze activities and dictation sentences for every Core Word 1–1200 providing extensive review of words and skills and expansion of writing. Teachers in grades 1–6 may also want their grade-level ***Word-Wise Sourcebook***, the laugh-aloud rhymes for learning language skills.

How are activities selected?

There are far more activities included in ***Spelling Sourcebooks 2, 3,*** and ***4*** than any teacher should consider using. Instead, teachers are empowered to make strategic activity selections. Teachers can begin customizing their program through a determination of which activities will be taught and to whom. In the ***Sourcebook*** margins next to each activity, the skills developed within the activity are listed so that it is easy to identify specific areas for instruction and practice. Any activity could be used in a variety of formats—a teacher-directed exercise, homework project, a cooperative learning group activity, etc. Some teachers may wish to make the activity selections with their grade-level colleagues. This would provide greater program conformity. The ***Sourcebook*** activity selections should be made to balance the total language curriculum complementing any reading and language program currently in place.

A teacher may select two activities for whole-group, teacher-directed instruction. One of the activities might be labeled in the margin as a structural analysis activity in which students are brainstorming for words that follow the same rhyming letter pattern of the Core Word. The second whole-group, teacher-directed activity could be a literature book tie-in with another Core Word with a follow-up writing project.

Then three independent activities may be assigned to the class over the next few days—perhaps a phonics awareness exercise that requires students to find and write words with the same ending sound as a Core Word, a vocabulary activity in which students are listing synonyms for a Core Word, and a sentence-writing exercise related to another Core Word in the unit. These activities could be completed in class or taken home for homework. Completed assignments could be handed in to the teacher for correction, or corrected and discussed in class.

Additional activities could be assigned to students who need a challenge. These activities would be ones that the teacher views as more difficult. They may involve some research, such as exploring word origins. Often they would furnish more opportunities to write and think. After completing these activities, the students should be asked to share the products of their extension work with the class for the benefit of all students.

What are the different kinds of activities that teachers can select to customize their teaching?

Perhaps the greatest strength of the Core Word activity options is their number and variety. To generalize, the Core Word activity options are firmly founded in language experiences. Their use integrates spelling with language learning across the curriculum. All the traditional skills are included with their application being the focus. Following is a sampling of the activity idea options in ***Spelling Sourcebooks 2, 3,*** and ***4:***

literature—books and follow-up activities that reinforce and extend the Core Words

writing—motivational writing ideas that require students to apply their spelling skills in motivational writing activities

vocabulary building—activities that "springboard" from the Core Words to introduce other forms of the words, synonyms, antonyms, homophones, homographs, prefixes and suffixes, roots, multiple meanings, clipped words (*plane/airplane*), and words often confused (*then/than*)

visual activities—visual discrimination and perception activities, such as look-alike word games, word search puzzles, word shape exercises, and finding words in words

word origins—activities that encourage an understanding of word histories, eponyms, and foreign words and phrases

dictionary skills—activities that promote competent use of dictionaries and other writing references, including lessons on alphabetical order, multiple meanings, pronunciations, and syllabication

phonics—activities that reinforce sound-symbol correspondence; familiarity with silent letters; phonemic awareness; phonics rules and generalizations

structural analysis—activities for exploring compounds, contractions, double letters, and palindromes; affixes and word parts; and patterning activities

thinking skills—activities that help students explore word relationships through sequencing, analogies, and sorting; exercises that encourage students to discover multiple meanings of words; and creative and expository writing

spelling rules—activities that teach reliable rules, or generalizations, with opportunities to apply the rules to new words

What is the time frame for Core Word units?

The time frame for these activities varies from teacher to teacher and from unit to unit. This is because each teacher decides how many Core Words should be included in each unit and how many activities to include in each unit. The number of Core Words and the number of activities need not be the same for each unit. Units never need to begin on Monday and end on Friday. The traditional Monday-through-Friday time frame for spelling units is not supported by research. Research confirms that the best learning environment for spelling instruction is a flexible time frame that meets the needs of the student learners. All the better for busy teachers. So units can begin on *any day* with the preview, activities can follow for a few days, and then the unit can be closed on *any day* with the review. This flexibility parallels good teaching in reading, as well as the content areas.

How are units brought to a close?

A Core Word review brings closure to a unit (see Article 4, page 21). The format for the review is flexible. A review can repeat the preview process. This format is helpful to students who had difficulty on the preview. With this format, the review reinforces visual skill-building development. The words on the review are the same words that were presented on the preview, or additional previously introduced Core Words could be included.

Some teachers prefer to use another format for review. In addition to, or instead of a repeat of the preview, teachers can review skills and concepts taught through the activities they chose to do during the unit. For example, if the unit included a lesson on the plural rule for vowel-y and consonant-y word endings, then the review might ask students to write the plurals for new words that illustrate this plural rule.

What are the ***Spelling Sourcebook*** *Reviews?*

The most popular format for the review employs the ***Sourcebook Reviews.*** The ***Reviews*** are cloze and dictation activities for a current set of five Core Words. Previously introduced Core Words and skills are recycled through these activities. Teachers can give both the cloze exercise (on a blackline master) and the dictation, or either of the two. However, the opportunity for review suggests employing both. Further, student performance on these activities can contribute to the students' grades.

Are students accountable for the Core Words following each unit?

The Core Words are introduced routinely within a flexible time frame for the purpose of teaching and practicing spelling and proofreading skills and concepts. During a Core Word unit, the Core Words should be spelled correctly in all the unit activities and on the end-of-unit review using the cloze and dictation sentences in the ***Sourcebook Reviews.*** These words and the skills and concepts they develop are then recycled through upcoming ***Sourcebook*** activities and ***Sourcebook Reviews*** over and over again. Each subsequent encounter with previously introduced Core Words reviews their spelling. There is a most conscientious recycling process for both words and skills through the ***Sourcebook*** activity options. These ongoing encounters, paired with experiences the students have with these words in their writing, build the foundation for long-term mastery.

Yet, ongoing activities with words with a conscientious recycling process will not produce a careful speller. Spelling literacy is achieved through a commitment to accountability for spelling in writing. So which words are students accountable for spelling correctly in their writing? Their Priority Words—and any topical words a teacher chooses to add for a particular assignment.

How is spelling accountability achieved?

The Priority Words are the high-frequency writing words for which students are accountable for spelling correctly in all their everyday writing (see Article 8, page 33, and Article 9, page 39). Student writing samples are randomly selected from across the curriculum to check the level of student commitment to their Priority Words. And it follows that the level of a student's commitment to the Priority Words figures prominently into his or her spelling grade (see Article 10, page 45). With student expectations in place and high grading standards for spelling priority words correctly all the time, accountability develops for these words, as well as for others.

Will the program provide enough spelling practice without a spelling book?

Perhaps the greatest flaw of the traditional programs is that they provided far too little practice with each word during the weekly unit to allow for transfer of words to writing. "Accountability" in the traditional sense meant spelling the words correctly on the posttest, or Friday Test. With the ***Spelling Sourcebook*** methodology, students practice spelling every day as they write across the curriculum. They are held accountable for the correct spelling of an increasing number of words in this writing as they develop as a writer. And though there is no Friday Test in the old sense, there *is a test every day* in writing. This is more practice than ever before.

To complement this everyday practice in writing, teachers routinely involve students in skill and concept development through the Springboard Activities in ***Sourcebooks 2, 3,*** and ***4*** that grow from their grade-level Core Words. The program provides more of these activities than a teacher could possibly use so that a selection can be made for meeting a variety of needs. The degree to which teachers use these activities corresponds to the practice needs of their students. The ***Word-Wise Sourcebooks*** provide another medium for practice. These materials feature laugh-aloud rhymes on blackline masters that focus on the idiosyncrasies of words and their use—all with motivating follow-up activities. Then, the ***Sourcebook Reviews*** provide repeated practice with carefully selected review Core Words and skills that are recycled again and again.

Do students ever learn their Core Words, or only their Priority Words?

The repeated exposure through these different ***Sourcebook*** mediums for practice of the Core Words results in faithful learning of the Core Words. In fact, the Springboard Words that grow from the Core Words and the Springboard Activities are learned by many students, too. The total practice afforded students through the ***Sourcebook*** methodology should be compared to the limited practice and exposure of the spelling words in the weekly word lists of the traditional programs. What happened to those words after the Friday Test?

It is unrealistic to think that the only words students learn are the limited list of Priority Words. These words simply serve as base-line accountability for writing—spelling accountability can never fall below this basic requirement for a top grade. And indeed it shouldn't. It is inadmissible to reward students for exemplary spelling when fundamental spelling skills are lacking in their everyday writing for the most basic, high-use words.

Can parts of the program meet special learning needs?

More spelling practice can be provided through the Individualized List (see Article 11, page 49). Here students can choose their own words, parents can choose words, and teachers can add words. The Individualized list tailors spelling to specific student needs and interests.

Some students who are challenged by spelling can benefit from additional help developing the dominant modality for spelling growth—the visual modality. The program provides for this and other special needs (see Article 7, page 29, and Article 13, page 53). Students who are immensely capable spellers also need personalized consideration to meet their increased capabilities (see Article 12, page 51).

Of course, teachers may make some mistakes as they launch the ***Spelling Sourcebook*** methodology. So be it. The only way to avoid making a mistake is to do nothing—and that is the only unacceptable error. Considering that the traditional spelling programs reduced spelling instruction to an isolated subject unrelated to writing, any effort to implement a program that bonds spelling and writing is worth making a mistake or two during its implementation.

If questions arise, how can answers be found?

So, as the new program is implemented, teachers should anticipate temporary challenges. The problems are likely to be minor ones, easily solved by rereading the appropriate Articles in ***Spelling Sourcebook 1*** and reviewing the fast-paced staff development videos, "Introduction to Teachers" and "Management and Record Keeping Options" (both 70 minutes long available from Northwest Textbook). New understandings develop with each review. But, if a persistent question creates an obstacle because an answer cannot be found, the ***Spelling Sourcebook's*** author offers her help. Her home phone number is in the opening letter of every ***Spelling Sourcebook***. Call her. She is committed to helping dedicated teachers make the necessary changes to provide for spelling literacy in all students' writing. It is a change well worth making . . . and the change is overdue. The time to start is now.

Word Bank of 1200 High-Frequency Writing Words

Researchers over the years have carefully tabulated the highest-utility writing words. There are only minor differences in word placement among the most respected and massive studies, which serves to validate the totality of this research. The ***Spelling Sourcebook*** word bank of 1200 high-use writing words is a cross-referenced compilation of these word-frequency studies. At its base is the American Heritage Word Frequency Study (Carroll, Davies, Richman). However, several other valid studies significantly influenced the development of the word bank. These include the work of Gates, Horn, Rinsland, Greene and Loomer, Harris and Jacobson.

Between frequencies 1-999, all words have been included in the ***Spelling Sourcebook*** word bank, regardless of their phonetic complexity. For frequencies 1000-1200, words have been edited to make the word bank instructionally appropriate at the upper grade levels. Regularly spelled words with few letters have been omitted from the word bank within these frequencies. In their place are the next words that occur consecutively in the frequency studies. This maintains the integrity and consistency of the ***Spelling Sourcebook*** word bank, accurately indicating the relative frequency of use of the words listed. As a result, the word bank provides appropriate spelling words for the lower, as well as the upper grade levels.

This word bank is the source for the Core Words (see Article 2, page 9) and Priority Words (see Article 8, page 33, and Article 9, page 39). The words in the bank are listed in the order of their frequency of use in everyday writing. Words decrease in writing utility as the word numbers increase. Since *the* is the most frequently used word in our language, its number is one (1) in the word bank. Therefore, knowing how to spell *the* should provide a writer with more spelling power than knowing how to spell any other word, save the writer's own name.

frequency	word	frequency	word	frequency	word	frequency	word	frequency	word
1	the	49	how	97	just	145	number	193	want
2	of	50	up	98	where	146	great	194	school
3	and	51	out	99	most	147	tell	195	important
4	a	52	them	100	know	148	men	196	until
5	to	53	then	101	get	149	say	197	form
6	in	54	she	102	through	150	small	198	food
7	is	55	many	103	back	151	every	199	keep
8	you	56	some	104	much	152	found	200	children
9	that	57	so	105	go	153	still	201	feet
10	it	58	these	106	good	154	between	202	land
11	he	59	would	107	new	155	name	203	side
12	for	60	other	108	write	156	should	204	without
13	was	61	into	109	our	157	home	205	boy
14	on	62	has	110	me	158	big	206	once
15	are	63	more	111	man	159	give	207	animal
16	as	64	her	112	too	160	air	208	life
17	with	65	two	113	any	161	line	209	enough
18	his	66	like	114	day	162	set	210	took
19	they	67	him	115	same	163	own	211	four
20	at	68	see	116	right	164	under	212	head
21	be	69	time	117	look	165	read	213	above
22	this	70	could	118	think	166	last	214	kind
23	from	71	no	119	also	167	never	215	began
24	I	72	make	120	around	168	us	216	almost
25	have	73	than	121	another	169	left	217	live
26	or	74	first	122	came	170	end	218	page
27	by	75	been	123	come	171	along	219	got
28	one	76	its	124	work	172	while	220	earth
29	had	77	who	125	three	173	might	221	need
30	not	78	now	126	must	174	next	222	far
31	but	79	people	127	because	175	sound	223	hand
32	what	80	my	128	does	176	below	224	high
33	all	81	made	129	part	177	saw	225	year
34	were	82	over	130	even	178	something	226	mother
35	when	83	did	131	place	179	thought	227	light
36	we	84	down	132	well	180	both	228	country
37	there	85	only	133	such	181	few	229	father
38	can	86	way	134	here	182	those	230	let
39	an	87	find	135	take	183	always	231	night
40	your	88	use	136	why	184	show	232	picture
41	which	89	may	137	help	185	large	233	being
42	their	90	water	138	put	186	often	234	study
43	said	91	long	139	different	187	together	235	second
44	if	92	little	140	away	188	asked	236	soon
45	do	93	very	141	again	189	house	237	story
46	will	94	after	142	off	190	don't	238	since
47	each	95	words	143	went	191	world	239	white
48	about	96	called	144	old	192	going	240	ever

frequency	word
241	paper
242	hard
243	near
244	sentence
245	better
246	best
247	across
248	during
249	today
250	however
251	sure
252	knew
253	it's
254	try
255	told
256	young
257	sun
258	thing
259	whole
260	hear
261	example
262	heard
263	several
264	change
265	answer
266	room
267	sea
268	against
269	top
270	turned
271	learn
272	point
273	city
274	play
275	toward
276	five
277	himself
278	usually
279	money
280	seen
281	didn't
282	car
283	morning
284	I'm
285	body
286	upon
287	family
288	later

frequency	word
289	turn
290	move
291	face
292	door
293	cut
294	done
295	group
296	true
297	half
298	red
299	fish
300	plants
301	living
302	black
303	eat
304	short
305	United States
306	run
307	book
308	gave
309	order
310	open
311	ground
312	cold
313	really
314	table
315	remember
316	tree
317	course
318	front
319	American
320	space
321	inside
322	ago
323	sad
324	early
325	I'll
326	learned
327	brought
328	close
329	nothing
330	though
331	idea
332	before
333	lived
334	became
335	add
336	become

frequency	word
337	grow
338	draw
339	yet
340	less
341	wind
342	behind
343	cannot
344	letter
345	among
346	able
347	dog
348	shown
349	mean
350	English
351	rest
352	perhaps
353	certain
354	six
355	feel
356	fire
357	ready
358	green
359	yes
360	built
361	special
362	ran
363	full
364	town
365	complete
366	oh
367	person
368	hot
369	anything
370	hold
371	state
372	list
373	stood
374	hundred
375	ten
376	fast
377	felt
378	kept
379	notice
380	can't
381	strong
382	voice
383	probably
384	area

frequency	word
385	horse
386	matter
387	stand
388	box
389	start
390	that's
391	class
392	piece
393	surface
394	river
395	common
396	stop
397	am
398	talk
399	whether
400	fine
401	round
402	dark
403	past
404	ball
405	girl
406	road
407	blue
408	instead
409	either
410	held
411	already
412	warm
413	gone
414	finally
415	summer
416	understand
417	moon
418	animals
419	mind
420	outside
421	power
422	problem
423	longer
424	winter
425	deep
426	heavy
427	carefully
428	follow
429	beautiful
430	everyone
431	leave
432	everything

frequency	word
433	game
434	system
435	bring
436	watch
437	shell
438	dry
439	within
440	floor
441	ice
442	ship
443	themselves
444	begin
445	fact
446	third
447	quite
448	carry
449	distance
450	although
451	sat
452	possible
453	heart
454	real
455	simple
456	snow
457	rain
458	suddenly
459	easy
460	leaves
461	lay
462	size
463	wild
464	weather
465	miss
466	pattern
467	sky
468	walked
469	main
470	someone
471	center
472	field
473	stay
474	itself
475	boat
476	question
477	wide
478	least
479	tiny
480	hour

frequency	word	frequency	word	frequency	word	frequency	word	frequency	word
481	happened	529	bird	577	woman	625	yellow	673	wife
482	foot	530	wood	578	eye	626	party	674	island
483	care	531	color	579	milk	627	force	675	we'll
484	low	532	war	580	choose	628	test	676	opposite
485	else	533	fly	581	north	629	bad	677	born
486	gold	534	yourself	582	seven	630	temperature	678	sense
487	build	535	seem	583	famous	631	pair	679	cattle
488	glass	536	thus	584	late	632	ahead	680	million
489	rock	537	square	585	pay	633	wrong	681	anyone
490	tall	538	moment	586	sleep	634	practice	682	rule
491	alone	539	teacher	587	iron	635	sand	683	science
492	bottom	540	happy	588	trouble	636	tail	684	afraid
493	check	541	bright	589	store	637	wait	685	women
494	reading	542	sent	590	beside	638	difficult	686	produce
495	fall	543	present	591	oil	639	general	687	pull
496	poor	544	plan	592	modern	640	cover	688	son
497	map	545	rather	593	fun	641	material	689	meant
498	friend	546	length	594	catch	642	isn't	690	broken
499	language	547	speed	595	business	643	thousand	691	interest
500	job	548	machine	596	reach	644	sign	692	chance
501	music	549	information	597	lot	645	guess	693	thick
502	buy	550	except	598	won't	646	forward	694	sight
503	window	551	figure	599	case	647	huge	695	pretty
504	mark	552	you're	600	speak	648	ride	696	train
505	heat	553	free	601	shape	649	region	697	fresh
506	grew	554	fell	602	eight	650	nor	698	drive
507	listen	555	suppose	603	edge	651	period	699	lead
508	ask	556	natural	604	soft	652	blood	700	break
509	single	557	ocean	605	village	653	rich	701	sit
510	clear	558	government	606	object	654	team	702	bought
511	energy	559	baby	607	age	655	corner	703	radio
512	week	560	grass	608	minute	656	cat	704	method
513	explain	561	plane	609	wall	657	amount	705	king
514	lost	562	street	610	meet	658	garden	706	similar
515	spring	563	couldn't	611	record	659	led	707	return
516	travel	564	reason	612	copy	660	note	708	corn
517	wrote	565	difference	613	forest	661	various	709	decide
518	farm	566	maybe	614	especially	662	race	710	position
519	circle	567	history	615	necessary	663	bit	711	bear
520	whose	568	mouth	616	he's	664	result	712	hope
521	correct	569	middle	617	unit	665	brother	713	song
522	bed	570	step	618	flat	666	addition	714	engine
523	measure	571	child	619	direction	667	doesn't	715	board
524	straight	572	strange	620	south	668	dead	716	control
525	base	573	wish	621	subject	669	weight	717	spread
526	mountain	574	soil	622	skin	670	thin	718	evening
527	caught	575	human	623	wasn't	671	stone	719	brown
528	hair	576	trip	624	I've	672	hit	720	clean

frequency	word	frequency	word	frequency	word	frequency	word	frequency	word
721	wouldn't	769	wear	817	path	865	clothes	913	northern
722	section	770	act	818	careful	866	doctor	914	flower
723	spent	771	hat	819	narrow	867	indeed	915	star
724	ring	772	arm	820	mental	868	dance	916	feed
725	teeth	773	believe	821	nine	869	church	917	wooden
726	quiet	774	major	822	useful	870	original	918	sort
727	ancient	775	gray	823	public	871	enjoy	919	develop
728	stick	776	wonder	824	according	872	string	920	shoulder
729	afternoon	777	include	825	steel	873	sister	921	variety
730	silver	778	describe	826	salt	874	familiar	922	season
731	nose	779	electric	827	speech	875	onto	923	share
732	century	780	sold	828	forth	876	imagine	924	jump
733	therefore	781	visit	829	nation	877	blow	925	regular
734	level	782	sheep	830	knowledge	878	quick	926	represent
735	you'll	783	I'd	831	appear	879	law	927	market
736	death	784	office	832	ate	880	lie	928	we're
737	hole	785	row	833	dinner	881	final	929	flew
738	coast	786	contain	834	hurt	882	rise	930	finger
739	cross	787	fit	835	spend	883	loud	931	expect
740	sharp	788	equal	836	experiment	884	fair	932	army
741	fight	789	value	837	touch	885	herself	933	cabin
742	capital	790	yard	838	drop	886	slow	934	camp
743	fill	791	beat	839	chair	887	noise	935	danger
744	deal	792	inch	840	east	888	statement	936	purpose
745	busy	793	sugar	841	separate	889	hungry	937	breakfast
746	beyond	794	key	842	truck	890	join	938	proper
747	send	795	product	843	sing	891	tube	939	coat
748	love	796	desert	844	column	892	rode	940	push
749	cool	797	bank	845	twice	893	empty	941	express
750	cause	798	farther	846	particular	894	twenty	942	shot
751	please	799	won	847	shop	895	broke	943	angry
752	meat	800	total	848	unless	896	nice	944	southern
753	lady	801	sell	849	spot	897	effect	945	dress
754	west	802	wire	850	neither	898	paid	946	bag
755	glad	803	rose	851	met	899	motion	947	proud
756	action	804	cotton	852	wheel	900	myself	948	neck
757	pass	805	spoke	853	none	901	divide	949	breath
758	type	806	rope	854	hill	902	supply	950	strength
759	attention	807	fear	855	television	903	laid	951	member
760	gas	808	shore	856	bill	904	dear	952	twelve
761	kitchen	809	throughout	857	solve	905	surprise	953	mine
762	pick	810	compare	858	pressure	906	gun	954	company
763	scale	811	movement	859	report	907	entire	955	current
764	basic	812	exercise	860	farmer	908	fruit	956	pound
765	happen	813	bread	861	count	909	crowd	957	valley
766	safe	814	process	862	trade	910	band	958	double
767	grown	815	nature	863	chief	911	wet	959	till
768	cost	816	apart	864	month	912	solid	960	match

frequency	word	frequency	word	frequency	word	frequency	word	frequency	word
961	average	1009	industry	1057	dangerous	1105	vegetable	1153	disease
962	die	1010	they're	1058	event	1106	parents	1154	construction
963	liquid	1011	beneath	1059	leader	1107	style	1155	motor
964	alive	1012	laugh	1060	peace	1108	education	1156	affect
965	stream	1013	groceries	1061	spelling	1109	required	1157	conversation
966	provide	1014	popular	1062	chapter	1110	political	1158	evidence
967	drink	1015	thank	1063	swimming	1111	daughter	1159	citizen
968	experience	1016	quarter	1064	opportunity	1112	individual	1160	environment
969	future	1017	climbed	1065	immediately	1113	progress	1161	influence
970	tomorrow	1018	continue	1066	favorite	1114	altogether	1162	cancel
971	drove	1019	potatoes	1067	settled	1115	activities	1163	audience
972	population	1020	receive	1068	telephone	1116	article	1164	apartment
973	finish	1021	design	1069	repeat	1117	equipment	1165	worse
974	station	1022	president	1070	prepare	1118	discuss	1166	transportation
975	shook	1023	charge	1071	instance	1119	healthy	1167	frozen
976	stage	1024	mistake	1072	avenue	1120	perfect	1168	waste
977	oxygen	1025	hospital	1073	newspaper	1121	recognize	1169	couple
978	poem	1026	remain	1074	actually	1122	frequently	1170	function
979	solution	1027	service	1075	employee	1123	character	1171	connect
980	burn	1028	increase	1076	review	1124	personal	1172	project
981	cent	1029	students	1077	convince	1125	disappear	1173	pronounce
982	electricity	1030	insects	1078	allowed	1126	success	1174	offered
983	everybody	1031	address	1079	nobody	1127	traffic	1175	apply
984	rate	1032	sincerely	1080	details	1128	yesterday	1176	improve
985	dust	1033	dollars	1081	muscles	1129	situation	1177	stomach
986	worth	1034	belong	1082	model	1130	realize	1178	collect
987	community	1035	bottle	1083	climate	1131	message	1179	prevent
988	captain	1036	flight	1084	coffee	1132	recently	1180	courage
989	bus	1037	forget	1085	whenever	1133	account	1181	occur
990	protect	1038	bicycle	1086	serious	1134	physical	1182	foreign
991	cook	1039	secret	1087	angle	1135	neighbor	1183	quality
992	raise	1040	soldier	1088	feather	1136	excited	1184	terrible
993	further	1041	silent	1089	determined	1137	whisper	1185	instrument
994	steam	1042	structure	1090	dictionary	1138	available	1186	balance
995	guide	1043	height	1091	ordinary	1139	college	1187	ability
996	discover	1044	observe	1092	extra	1140	furniture	1188	arrange
997	plain	1045	indicate	1093	rough	1141	leather	1189	rhythm
998	usual	1046	railroad	1094	library	1142	husband	1190	avoid
999	seat	1047	knife	1095	condition	1143	principal	1191	daily
1000	accept	1048	married	1096	arrived	1144	medicine	1192	identity
1001	police	1049	suggested	1097	located	1145	excellent	1193	standard
1002	consider	1050	entered	1098	program	1146	operation	1194	combine
1003	dozen	1051	magazine	1099	pencil	1147	council	1195	attached
1004	baseball	1052	agree	1100	tongue	1148	author	1196	frighten
1005	rubber	1053	fifty	1101	title	1149	organize	1197	social
1006	symbol	1054	escape	1102	enemy	1150	concern	1198	factory
1007	support	1055	threw	1103	garage	1151	barbecue	1199	license
1008	exactly	1056	planet	1104	lose	1152	accident	1200	recommend

Research Review: Practices Supported By Research

The-test-study-test method of instruction
This method is superior to study-test methodology.

The self-corrected test procedure
The single most important factor contributing to spelling success is the administration of a pretest in which the students correct their own tests with teacher guidance.

A comparison of pretest and posttest results
Students should maintain their own performance records, set goals for themselves, and note progress.

An independent word-study procedure
Students who utilize a multi-modality independent word-study procedure become more capable spellers than students who do not.

Focus on high-use writing vocabulary
Spelling is a subskill of writing and should therefore emphasize words needed in everyday writing.

Spelling those words the students already know and understand
Students should have mastered through listening, speaking, and reading those words identified for spelling instruction.

Words presented in list form
Words for study should initially be presented in a list, as opposed to sentence or paragraph form.

Words presented as whole words
Words should be presented as whole words, instead of in syllables.

Words presented in print
When words are presented in print, students can more easily form and retain a correct visual image of the words.

No premarking of hard words or hard parts of words
Predetermining for students the words or parts of words that may be difficult for them causes more difficulty in mastering those words in daily writing.

Rules limited to those of high utility
There are very few spelling rules that provide the students with valid spelling direction. Rules must be carefully selected so that they apply to a large number of words, have few exceptions, and are easy to remember.

Use of brief daily structured-practice sessions
Structured practice should be limited to 10—15 minutes daily.

Practice that provides for multiple writings of the words
In order to internalize their spelling words for transference into daily writing, students need many opportunities to write the words in various kinds of activities.

Ample opportunities to use the words in daily writing
Spelling is for writing, and spelling instruction must include abundant practice within the writing process.

Use of related language skills only as an aid to spelling
Such related language skills as phonics, dictionary practice, structural analysis, handwriting, parts of speech, etc, must never take precedence over spelling as students initially study their words.

Use of in-context writing for spelling assessment
The only valid indicator of spelling success is consistent use of correctly spelled words in a writer's everyday writing. Authentic spelling assessment must mirror the use of spelling in the real world.

Research Review: Practices Not Supported By Research

The study-test method of instruction
This method should be eliminated in favor of the test-study-test method.

Use of a midweek pretest corrected by the teacher
A self-corrected pretest guided by the teacher prior to word study constitutes the single most important factor contributing to spelling success.

Select words based on their phonetic or structural properties
Words should be selected based on their frequency in writing first. Then they should be grouped to reflect a mix of sounds and patterns to encourage observation of the likenesses and differences of words.

Use of words being studied for vocabulary expansion
Words taught for spelling should be words students have already mastered in listening, speaking, and reading comprehension. They should not be words students are learning to read and understand.

Feature words from content areas
Words should not be derived from other curricular areas unless they are high-frequency writing words.

Words initially presented in syllables or structural parts
Learning to spell a word involves forming a correct visual image of the whole word. All words should be introduced as whole words so that students can more easily form and retain correct visual images of them.

Words presented in cursive handwriting
Students are better able to form and retain a correct visual image of a word if it is presented in printing.

Hard words or hard parts of words clearly marked
Predetermining for students possible spelling difficulties *creates* spelling difficulties rather than alleviates them.

Teach every spelling rule
Rules should be carefully selected and then taught through exposure to their exemplars over time. Very few rules provide valid spelling direction.

Copy words multiple times for spelling practice
Repeated writings of words without intervening attempts at recall should not be required. Productive practice must involve spelling the word from memory, not just copying it.

Write words in the air
It is more productive to write the words on paper.

Teach spelling in large, weekly blocks of time
Spelling is best taught 10–15 minutes daily.

Emphasize related language skills
Spelling must ultimately be integrated with related language skills, but during the initial study of the words, an emphasis on peripheral skills will hinder spelling acquisition.

Teach spelling solely through practice exercises
Practice exercises help students learn the letter sequences of words and internalize them for transference into daily writing. However, a total program also offers abundant opportunities for using the words in daily writing.

Emphasize oral spelling drills
Spelling is a subskill of writing and is best reinforced through the writing of words.

Assess spelling on a test of words in isolation
Spelling ability can never be authentically assessed apart from real, everyday writing.

Spelling Rules

Very few spelling rules, or generalizations, are effective in teaching spelling. For a rule to be valid, it must apply to a large number of words and have few exceptions. Following are rules that meet these criteria.

Suffixes

Double the Final Consonant
Double the final consonant of a word that ends with a single vowel and consonant before adding a suffix that begins with a vowel. (*get/getting*)

Double the final consonant of a word that is accented on the final syllable and ends with a single vowel and consonant before adding a suffix that begins with a vowel. (*permit/permitted*)

Words Ending in Silent *e*
Drop the final silent *e* before adding a suffix that begins with a vowel. (*have/having*)

Keep the final silent *e* when adding a suffix that begins with a consonant. (*late/lately*)

Words Ending in *y*
Change the *y* to *i* when adding a suffix to words that end in consonant *-y,* unless the suffix begins with *i.* (*try/tried*)

Do not change the *y* to *i* when adding a suffix to words that end in vowel *-y.* (*play/played*)

Plurals

Add *s* to most nouns to form plurals. (*friend/friends*)

Add *es* to nouns that end with *s, ss, sh, ch,* or *x.* (*box/boxes, class/classes*)

Change the *y* to *i* and add *es* to nouns that end in consonant *-y.* (*country/countries*)

Add *s* to nouns that end in vowel *-y.* (*key/keys*)

Change the *f* or *fe* to *v* and add *es* to some nouns that end in *f* or *fe.* (*half/halves, knife/knives*)

Some nouns change their spellings to form the plural. (*foot/feet*)

Some nouns are spelled the same for both singular and plural. (*sheep*)

Spelling Games & Activities

Motivational games and activities can reinforce spelling and related language skills by creating an easy-to-learn format for practice. Following are examples of activities that can complement the Core Curriculum for spelling.

ABC Order

An activity for reinforcing alphabetical order

Prepare for the game by writing Core Words or their other word forms on cards. Place three word cards on each student's desk. Ask students to alphabetize their cards. As soon as students complete the task, quickly check their work. If the words are alphabetized correctly, give them another word card to alphabetize into the set. At any point in the game, if a student's words are not in correct ABC order, show the student the correct order. Then replace the word cards with three new cards.

The object of the game is to get as many cards as possible. This depends upon speed as well as alphabet accuracy. As a follow-up activity, ask students to write their list of alphabetized words. Winners can post their lists on the bulletin board.

ABC Order can be played in cooperative learning groups, too.

All in the Family

An activity for teaching other word forms of the Core Words

Prepare for the game by dividing students into cooperative learning groups. Each group needs paper and pencil.

Begin the game by calling out a Core Word. The first player in each group writes the word. The paper and pencil are passed to the next member of the group and a derivative, or other word form, of the word is written. Each successive player writes a derivative until the group can think of no more, or until time is up (about 3 minutes). One point is awarded for the correct spelling of the base word and each of the derivatives. The group with the most points at the end of the game wins. Or the whole class wins a prize when the point total for all groups combined reaches a certain number.

As a follow-up activity, ask students to write selected other word forms in sentences.

All-Play Spelling Bee

A Spelling Bee in which students are never eliminated from play

Prepare for the game by writing Core Words or their other word forms on cards, each with a short context sentence confirming the meaning of the word. Divide the players into two teams of equal spelling ability. Give each team an equal number of word cards (about twice as many cards as players).

The first player on the starting team selects any word card from the set, calls out the word, and reads it in the context sentence. The first player on the opposite team goes to the chalkboard and prints the word. Using the corrected-test procedure, the two players check the spelling. If the word is correctly spelled, the word card is eliminated from the game. If the word is misspelled, it is written correctly, erased, and the word card is returned to the pile.

Players are never eliminated from the game, only word cards are eliminated. The first team to eliminate the opposite team's word cards wins.

Bingo

A spelling activity that parallels the traditional number bingo game

Prepare for the game by showing students how to fold a piece of writing paper into 16 boxes (4 folds). Ask students to select spelling words from a list of about 20 words to print in the boxes of their paper. Words can be used only once in the boxes. Some words will not be used.

Decide which row or column will be *bingo*. Provide each student with a colored pencil, crayon, or pen.

Begin the game by calling out a spelling word, using the word in a short sentence, and spelling and printing the word on the chalkboard (a student volunteer could spell and print the word on the chalkboard). If students have the word in a box on their *bingo* paper, they trace over the word with their writing utensil as it is spelled. If they do not, they turn the paper over and print the word on the back of the paper as it is spelled.

The first student to get *bingo* wins, but play can continue until all words have been used. For shorter or longer *bingo* games, adjust the number of folds that make the word boxes.

This game could be played using only words that have homophone partners. For follow up, have students write the homophone partners and use designated homophones in context sentences to confirm their meaning. Or the game could be played using only words that have opposite partners. For follow up, have students write the opposite partners and use designated sets of words in sentences. Another variation is to use only words that have synonyms. Then, after the game have students list a synonym for each of the words in their *bingo* game. To reinforce prefixes and/or suffixes, use only words to which a prefix or a suffix could be added. Then have students add the affixes following the *bingo* game.

Contractions could be used exclusively in the game. Then follow up with students writing the longer forms of the words.

To play Compound Bingo, write half of each compound word in a different column on the chalkboard. Have students make compound words out of the two word parts to write in their *bingo* boxes. After the *bingo* game, ask students to recombine the compound word parts to make new words.

Connect the Dots

An activity for reinforcing Core Words

Prepare for the game by providing each pair of students with a game sheet. This sheet is a teacher-made blackline master of 16 dots arranged in rows of four to form a square (adjust the number of dots for longer or shorter games). The players need a list of their Core Words to be used in the game, paper, and pencil.

The first player selects a spelling word, pronounces it, and uses it in a short context sentence to confirm its meaning. The other player prints the word on the paper from memory. Using the corrected-test procedure, the players check the spelling of the word. If the word is correct, the player who spelled the word correctly may connect two adjacent dots on the game sheet. Roles then reverse, and play continues.

The object of the game is to form squares by connecting dots on the game sheet. For a sixteen-dot game sheet, nine squares can be formed. The player to draw the last line to form any square on the game sheet writes his or her name in that square. The player with the most squares at the end of the game wins.

Connect the Dots can also be played by teams using a game board drawn on the chalkboard.

Finish the Story

A creative activity that reinforces correct spelling in writing

Prepare for the game by writing the words to be practiced on the chalkboard. These can be current Core Words, Springboard Words, or tricky review words, such as homophones. Place students in cooperative learning groups. Each group needs a paper and a pencil.

Begin telling a story while the students listen. Then have the students work cooperatively in their groups to finish writing the story using as many of the words on the chalkboard in their story as they can. Set a timer. When the bell rings (10-12 minutes), the students exchange their stories with another group for proofreading. Each group reports on errors they found and corrected. Then the stories are returned to the original group for class sharing.

Letter Grid Games

Activities that help promote the development of visual skills

Prepare for the games by duplicating a blackline-master grid (read about Blackline Master 4 in Blackline Master Resources, page 98). Each student needs a copy of a grid. Students can reinforce visual skills through grid activities by focusing attention on each individual letter as a unit in a spelling word, rather than seeing the word as a reader would.

Students can write the Core Words in the grid using each box for a letter, with tall letters extending to the upper row of boxes and tail letters to the lower row of boxes. Then students can draw a line around the letters to emphasize the visual shape of the word.

Students can make a word-search puzzle in the grid for a partner to complete. Words should be written in a word search from left to right or top to bottom.

Students can create crossword puzzles in the grid with written word clues for a partner to complete.

During all grid activities, students should further reinforce their words by turning their paper over and writing the words again. For example, after each word has been found in a word-search puzzle, students can write the word from memory on the flip side of the grid.

Mr. Pickyfood

A thinking activity that reinforces word properties

Prepare for the game by writing on the chalkboard the headings, LIKES and DOESN'T LIKE. Introduce the class to Mr. Pickyfood, a man who only eats what he likes. In the LIKES column write *peas, popcorn,* and *pumpkin pie.* In the DOESN'T LIKE column write *jam, beans,* and *french fries.* Let students volunteer to suggest a food to see if it is one Mr. Pickyfood likes to eat. If the food begins with the letter *p,* ask the student to write it in the LIKES column. All other suggestions are written in the DOESN'T LIKE list. Offer spelling assistance as necessary.

The object of the game is to discover the pattern in Mr. Pickyfood's pickiness (he only likes foods that begin with the letter *p*). Other foods to Mr. Pickyfood's liking might include *pizza, potatoes, peanut butter, peaches, pasta, pot roast, pineapple, pepper,* and *pickles.*

Mr. Pickyfood can be played using various patterns in his pickiness, such as foods with the long *e* sound, double letters, or five letters. Mr. Pickyfood has some picky cousins that make for entertaining word games, too. They are Miss Pickywear (clothes), Mrs. Pickypet (animals), and Mr. Pickypack (travel items).

But this game can also be played without a subject theme. Then call the game Mr. and Mrs. Picky. When students volunteer to write a word on the board, tell them whether it should be written in the LIKES or DOESN'T LIKE column. See how long it takes the students to guess the pattern. Categories might be words with suffixes and without suffixes, words with opposites and without opposites, or nouns and non-nouns. Once the students have correctly identified the pattern, have them continue the game, independently writing a LIKES and DOESN'T LIKE list to complement the class list on the chalkboard.

Mystery Words

A cloze activity that reinforces spelling and usage skills

Prepare for the activity by creating a paragraph or short story on a current topic of student interest. Write the story on the chalkboard or on a blackline master. Leave blanks for selected words or letters in words. Students complete the activity by providing the missing words or letters.

Or make a copy of a short story, paragraph, or poem from printed material. Use a typist's "white out" to remove selected words or letters in words. Place a number in the margin for each of these omitted words or letters. Then recopy and duplicate. Students read the selection and complete the activity by providing the missing words or letters. Their answers should be written on separate paper beside the appropriate number. Or students could rewrite the whole selection.

Mystery Words provides an excellent format to practice correct homophone usage.

Password

A thinking and spelling activity that resembles TV's Password

Prepare for the game by writing selected Core Words or their other word forms on cards. Two pairs of students play this game. Each pair is given a different set of word cards. The team pairs take turns providing synonyms or word clues to their partner to guess the words on the word cards. Guessing sessions are timed. A team is awarded a point for each word guessed within the time limit. After the timing, another point can be earned if the word guessed can be correctly written on the chalkboard. After each team has played, the team with the most points wins.

Prefix/Suffix Boxes

An activity that expands spelling and vocabulary through affixes

Prepare for the game by making a square divided into nine equal boxes. Make copies of this box to use for future Prefix/Suffix Boxes games. For Prefix Boxes, label each row with a different prefix. Label each column with an ending letter of a word. Students fill in the boxes with a word that begins with with the appropriate prefix and ends with the appropriate letter. For Suffix Boxes, label each row with a beginning letter for a word. Label each column with a suffix. Students fill in the boxes with a word that begins with the appropriate letter and ends with the appropriate suffix.

Students can share their games to make a cumulative list of correct responses for each box.

Questions and Answers

An activity that promotes spelling in writing

Prepare for the game by asking students to write each of their Core Words in an interrogative, or question, sentence. Ask them to leave three lines between each question. Collect the sentences and redistribute them making sure that students do not get their own questions. Then ask students to respond to the questions they were given in the space provided on the paper. Each response must use the spelling word in the reply.

Variations of this game include beginning with the answer statements for which students later write the questions; and writing sentences which students later rewrite, changing the tense of each sentence.

Race Track Spelling

A competitive activity that reinforces spelling skills

Prepare for the game by creating a "race track" on a large bulletin board. The race track consists of four long strips of construction paper of equal length (each a separate track) with about 15 spaces marked on each track.

Divide the class into four teams. Ask each team to make a small race car of construction paper and name it. Pin each race car to the starting line for one of the four tracks.

Play begins by asking one team member from each team to spell the same word. This can be done on paper, individual slate boards, or on the class chalkboard divided so that players cannot see the word of their opponents.

Each player spelling a word correctly may advance the team race car one space. Play continues with team members spelling words until one race car crosses the finish line. That team is the winner.

This game can be an ongoing one in which play takes place for brief periods each day. The number of race track boxes can be increased for longer games.

Variations of this game include Climb the Ladder, in which team members compete to climb each step of a ladder, Go to the Moon, in which a moon is the destination that spaceships are trying to reach along a vertical course, or Surfrider, which uses wave peaks as spaces to advance toward shore.

Red and Green

An active spelling game

Prepare for the game by placing students in circles with at least six students to a circle. A leader sits in the center of each circle, eyes closed, with a list of spelling words. A paper and a pencil are also in the center of each circle.

The leader calls "Green," and the students pass an object (bean bag, ball, bottle cap) clockwise around the circle. When the leader calls "Red," the object stops. The student holding the object when red is called is "it." The leader, now with eyes open, reads a spelling word from the list, uses it in a sentence, then calls "Green." At this, "it" passes the object on, darts to the center of the circle, and prints the spelling word on the paper. When the object has passed full circle and is back in the hands of the student to the left of "it's" place, that student calls "Red." "It" must then stop writing. If "it" spelled the word correctly before red was called, then "it" becomes the leader. If not, "it" returns to the outside of the circle, and play continues.

Sentence Puzzles

A spelling activity that parallels TV's Wheel of Fortune

Prepare for the game by asking students to independently write their spelling words in sentences. Check the sentences for spelling accuracy. Each student then chooses one sentence and, on another paper, makes word blanks for each word in the sentence, using a separate blank for each letter, and leaving a space between words. The student then fills in the first letter of each word. Divide the students into pairs. Each pair of students takes turns trying to determine their partner's sentence by asking for various letters to be filled in. The goal is to determine the sentence with the least number of letters requested for fill-in.

This game can also be played by teams or as a class activity by writing the sentence blanks on the chalkboard.

Sentence Spelling

A sentence dictation activity played in teams

Prepare for the game by dividing the players into groups and seating each group around a table. Each group needs one sheet of writing paper and one pencil.

Ask each group to write the same sentence. Say the sentence two times, then say "Begin."

The first player in each group writes the first word of the sentence and passes the sheet along to the next player. Each player writes one word until the sentence is complete. Players must write their words independently without benefit of any help from another player. The last player in sequence is the proofreader and may make any changes he or she wishes. As soon as the sentence is proofread, the proofreader stands up to signal that the team is done.

Sentences are checked and points are earned following these suggested guidelines:

1. Speed—The first team to correctly complete the sentence earns an extra five points.
2. Mechanics—One point for a capital at the beginning of the sentence and one for correct punctuation at the end. Additional points can be added for quotation marks, commas . . . whatever.
3. Spelling—One point for each correctly spelled word (any words with illegible letters do not earn points).

Spelling Baseball

A spelling game that parallels baseball

Prepare for the game by arranging the classroom to accommodate a baseball diamond—three bases and home plate. Write review Core Words and their other word forms on cards, each with a short context sentence to confirm word meaning. Divide the players into two teams. Determine how many innings there will be in the game.

The first team "at bat" sends their first player to the chalkboard. The first player on the opposite team "pitches" a word from the set of cards to the batter. The batter prints the word on the chalkboard. Then the word is checked using the self-corrected test procedure. If the word is correct, the batter advances to first base and the second batter continues the game, with the second player on the opposite team assuming the role of pitcher.

If a batter misses a word, it is an "out." Three outs and the opposite team is at bat. Points are scored by players crossing home plate—they advance one base for each word spelled correctly by a batter.

Play continues through the number of innings predetermined for the game.

Variations and follow-up activities for Spelling Baseball are the same as those for Bingo.

Spelling Boxes

An activity that reinforces Core Words and their other word forms

Prepare for the game by making a matrix, or grid. Make copies of the matrix to use for future Spelling Boxes games. Label each column with a word-form indicator, such as *ing, ed, plural, tion or sion, past tense, ly, base word, less, ment,* etc. Randomly fill in one word in each row. That word is the clue word for the row. Students fill in the empty boxes of each row with a form of the clue word, as indicated at the top of each column.

As the students complete the empty boxes, they may use a dictionary for help.

Some boxes can be starred. These boxes indicate words that must be used in a sentence on the reverse side of the paper.

Spelling Squares

A word-making activity

Prepare for the game by making a blackline master of a square divided into nine equal boxes in rows of three. Write a letter or group of letters in each box. Groups of letters should be ones often found in words, such as *ing, tion,* or *br.* Place a vowel in the center box and in one or two other boxes. Provide each student with a game sheet, pencil, and paper.

The object of the game is to write as many words as possible on the paper using the letters in the boxes. Words can be made by using letters in adjacent boxes only. Any letter can be doubled.

The game can be played individually, with each player using a different game sheet, or all players using the same game sheet. Spelling Squares can also be played in cooperative learning groups or as a brainstorming game for the whole class.

Word Sorts

A spelling activity that promotes thinking about word properties

Prepare for the game by writing a list of Core Words and Springboard Words on the chalkboard. Ask students to group, or sort, them in some way. Sorting options are endless and could involve parts of speech, alphabetical groupings, vowel sounds, affixes, structural characteristics, and so on.

Then ask selected students to write their word sorts on the chalkboard to see if others can identify their sorting system. Ask the remaining students to work in pairs to determine their partner's sorting system.

Write and Fold Relay

A team spelling activity

Prepare for the relay by dividing the class into teams. Each team needs one sheet of paper and a pencil. Arrange each team in a line behind a student desk. Place paper and pencil on each team's desk. Say a spelling word and use it in a sentence. Set a timer for a few seconds. Say "Go." The first player on each team hurries to the desk and prints the spelling word on the paper. When the timer rings, the players fold the paper horizontally so that the spelling word is folded under and return to their team. Play continues with each player taking a turn at the desk and printing another spelling word on the paper as it is said and used in a sentence. The team with the most correctly spelled words wins the game.

Vary this game by using only homophones, by having the players write the antonym for a given word, or by giving a sentence and having each player on a team write one word of the sentence.

5-7-10

An activity in which players spell for points

Prepare for the game by creating word cards of base forms of the Core Words. Write a 5 on the back of each of these cards. Then create word cards for the other word forms of the Core Words. Depending upon the spelling difficulty of these words, write a 7 or a 10 on the back (10 is most difficult). Pairs of students arrange their word cards face down into sets worth 5, 7, or 10. The players take turns asking their partner to draw a card from the pile of their choice. The partner pronounces the word on the word card and then uses it in a sentence. The other player prints the word. If the word is correct, the player keeps the card and scores the number of points indicated on the back. The object of the game is to have the most points when all the cards are gone.

Reference 5

Writing Motivators

Students must write every day. Following are ideas to add variety to students' writing. Ask students to create and write . . .

ads
advice columns
almanacs
analogies
announcements
applications
apologies
autobiographies
awards
beauty suggestions
bibliographies
billboards
biographies
birth certificates
book jackets
book reviews
books
bulletins
bumper stickers
buyer's guides
calendars
catalogs
campaign posters
campaign speeches
cartoons
chain letters
character sketches
charts
checklists
comic strips
comics
commercials
community newsletters
comparisons/contrasts
complaints
conversations
crossword puzzles
definitions
descriptions
diagrams
diaries
dictionaries
diets
directions
editorials
epitaphs
eponyms
essays
etymologies
evaluations
eyewitness accounts
explanations
expense reports
fables
fairy tales
fictional stories
folklore
footnotes
fortune cookie messages
games
ghost stories
gossip columns
graduation announcements
graffiti
greeting cards
grocery lists
headlines
histories
horoscope
how-to articles
idioms
indexes
inquiries
insults
interviews
invitations
itineraries
jeopardy questions
job applications
jokes
journals
jump rope rhymes
labels
laws
legends
letters
lists
loans
lyrics
magazines
mail order catalogs
maps
meeting minutes
memos
memoirs
metaphors
menus
monologues
movie reviews
musical messages
mysteries
myths
narratives
newscasts
newspapers
news releases
notices
nursery rhymes
obituaries
odes
opinions
palindromes
pamphlets
paragraphs
parenting tips
passports
persuasive articles
pictorials
picture captions
plays
pledges
poems
postcards
posters
problems
proposals
proverbs
purchase receipts
puppet shows
puns
puzzles
quips
quizzes
questionnaires
quotations
rationales
reasons
rebuttals
recipes
recommendations
recreational ideas
regulations
remedies
reports
requirements
resumes
reviews
riddles
rules
safety tips
sales brochures
sample lessons
schedules
science fiction
score cards
sentences
sequel stories
sermons
signs
silly sayings
slogans
songs
speeches
sports play-by-plays
summaries
superstitions
surveys
tall tales
telegrams
telephone directories
tests
thank you notes
titles
tombstones
tongue twisters
tourist attractions
travel folders
trivia
TV shows
valentines
vitae
want ads
wanted posters
warnings
weather forecasts/reports
welcomes
who's who
wills
wishes
word games
word lists
word lore
yearbooks
yellow pages

Bibliography

Baldwin, Ronald F. "The Effect of Teacher In-Service Training and Knowledge of Research on Spelling Instruction and Achievement of Elementary School Children." Ph.D. Thesis, University of Iowa, 1975

Barbe, Walter B., Azalia S. Francis, and Lois A. Braun, eds. *Spelling: Basic Skills for Effective Communication.* Columbus, OH: Zaner-Bloser, Inc., 1982.

Carroll, J. B., Peter Davies, and Barry Richman. *The American Heritage Word Frequency Book.* New York: Houghton Mifflin, 1971

Chomsky, Carol. "Reading, Writing, and Phonology." *Harvard Educational Review*, Vol. 40, May, 1970.

Chomsky, Noam, and Morris Halle. *The Sound Pattern of English.* New York: Harper and Row, 1968.

Cohen, Gloria Freeman. "A Developmental Study of Word Recognition Processes." Ed.D. Thesis, Rutgers, The State University of New Jersey, 1975.

Cohen, Leo A. "Evaluating Structural Analysis Methods Used in Spelling Books." Ed.D. Thesis, Boston University, 1969.

Culyer, Gail Blake. "A Synthesized Approach to Selecting Spelling Words and Generalizations." Ph. D. Thesis, The Florida State University, 1974

Dale, Edgar, and Joseph O'Rourke. *The Living Word Vocabulary.* Chicago: World Book-Childcraft International, Inc., 1981

DiStefano, Philip, and Patricia Hagerty. "Teaching Spelling at the Elementary Level," *The Reading Teacher,* Vol. 38, January, 1985.

Fitzsimmons, Robert J., and Bradley M. Loomer. *Spelling: The Research Basis.* Iowa City: The University of Iowa, 1980.

Flood, James, and Peter H. Salus. *Language and the Language Arts.* Englewood Cliffs, NJ: Prentice-Hall, Inc., 1984

Frith, Uta, ed. *Cognitive Processes in Spelling.* London: Academic Press, 1980.

Fry, Edward Bernard, Jacqueline K. Polk, and Dona Fountoukidis. *The Reading Teacher's Book of Lists.* Englewood Cliffs, NJ: Prentice-Hall, Inc., 1984.

Gates, Arthur I. *Generalization and Transfer in Spelling.* New York: Columbia University, 1935.

Gates, Arthur I. *Spelling Difficulties in 3,876 Words.* New York: Columbia University, 1937.

Gentry, J. Richard, and Edmund H. Henderson. "Three Steps to Teaching Beginning Readers to Spell." *The Reading Teacher,* Vol. 31, March, 1978.

Graham, Steve. "Evaluating Spelling Programs and Materials." *Teaching Exceptional Children.* Vol. 17, No. 4, Summer, 1985.

Graves, Donald H. "Research Update of Spelling Texts and Structural Analysis Methods." *Language Arts,* Vol. 54, No. 1. Urbana, IL: National Council of Teachers of English, 1977.

Greene, Henry A., and Bradley M. Loomer. *The New Iowa Spelling Scale.* Iowa City: The University of Iowa, 1977.

Haber, Ralph Norman, and Lyn R. Haber. "The Shape of a Word Can Specify Its Meaning." *Reading Research Quarterly,* Vol. XVI, No. 3. Newark, DE: International Reading Association, Inc., 1981.

Hagerty, Patricia. "Comparative Analysis of High Frequency Words Found in Commercial Spelling Series and Misspelled in Students' Writing to a Standard Measure of Word Frequency." Ed.D. Thesis, University of Colorado, 1981.

Hakanson, Edward Eric. "The Relationship Between Selected Visual and Auditory Perception Capacities and Spelling Capability as Measured by Tests Requiring Spelling Recognition and Spelling Recall." Ph.D. Thesis, University of Minnesota, 1966.

Hanna, Paul R., et al. *Phoneme-Grapheme Correspondences as Cues to Spelling Improvement.* Washington, DC: Government Printing Office, U.S. Office of Education, 1966.

Hanna, Paul R., Richard E. Hodges, and Jean S. Hanna. Spelling: Structure and Strategies. Boston: Houghton Mifflin, 1971.

Harp, Bill. "When the Principal Asks, 'Why Are Your Kids Giving Each Other Spelling Tests?'" *Reading Teacher,* Vol. 41, No. 7, March, 1988.

Harris, Albert J., and Milton Jacobson. Basic Elementary *Reading Vocabularies.* New York: Macmillan, 1972.

Henderson, Edmond H. *Teaching Spelling.* Boston: Houghton Mifflin, 1985.

Henderson, Edmund H. *Learning to Read and Spell.* DeKalb, IL: Northern Illinois University Press, 1981.

Henderson, Edmund H., and James W. Beers, eds. *Developmental and Cognitive Aspects of Learning to Spell: A Reflection of Word Knowledge.* Newark, DE: International Reading Association, Inc., 1980.

Henderson, Edmund H., and Shane Templeton. "A Developmental Perspective of Formal Spelling Instruction Through Alphabet, Pattern, and Meaning." *Elementary School Journal,* Vol. 66, No. 3, 1986.

Hillerich, Robert L. *Spelling: An Element of Written Expression.* Columbus, OH: Charles E. Merrill, Co., 1976.

Hillerich, Robert L. "Spelling: To Teach Not Just to Observe." *Illinois Schools Journal,* Vol. 66, No. 2, 1987.

Hodges, Richard E. *Learning to Spell.* Urbana, IL: ERIC Clearinghouse on Reading and Communication, 1981.

Horn, Ernest. *A Basic Writing Vocabulary: 10,000 Frequently Used Words in Writing.* Monograph First Series, No. 4. Iowa City: The University of Iowa, 1926.

Horn, Ernest. "Spelling." *Encyclopedia of Educational Research,* 3rd ed. New York: Macmillan, 1960.

Horn, Thomas. "The Effect of the Corrected Test on Learning to Spell." Master's Thesis, The University of Iowa, 1946.

Horn, Thomas. "The Effect of a Syllable Presentation of Words Upon Learning to Spell." Ph.D. Thesis, The University of Iowa, 1947.

Horn, Thomas. "Spelling." *Encyclopedia of Educational Research,* 4th ed. New York: Macmillan, 1969.

Horn, Thomas, and H. J. Otto. *Spelling Instruction: A Curriculum-Wide Approach.* Austin, TX: University of Texas, 1954.

Horsky, Gregory Alexander. "A Study of the Perception of Letters and Basic Sight Vocabulary Words of Fourth and Fifth Grade Children." Ph.D. Thesis, The University of Iowa, 1974.

Humphry, M. O. "The Effect of a Syllabic Presentation of Words Upon Learning to Spell." Master's Thesis, University of Texas, 1954.

Jacobson, Milton. "Foreward to Teacher's Edition." *Houghton Mifflin Spelling.* Houghton Mifflin, 1985.

Kingsley, J. H. "The Test-Study Method Versus Study-Test Method in Spelling." *Elementary School Journal,* Vol. 24. Chicago: The University of Chicago Press, 1923.

Larson, I. M. "Time Allotment in the Teaching of Spelling." Master's Thesis, University of Iowa, 1945.

Loomer, Bradley M. *Educator's Guide to Spelling Research and Practice.* Iowa City: The University of Iowa, Project Spelling, 1978.

Loomer, Bradley M. *The Most Commonly Asked Questions About Spelling . . . and What the Research Says.* North Billerica, MA: Curriculum Associates, 1982.

Lutz, Elaine. "ERIC/RCS Report: Invented Spelling and Spelling Development." *Language Arts,* Vol. 63, No. 7, November, 1986.

MacGregor, Sister Marilyn. "Multiple Regression Analysis of Essential Variables Contributing to Spelling Achievement." Ed.D. Thesis, Boston University School of Education, 1976.

Maheady, Larry, and Gregory F. Harper. "A Class-Wide Peer Tutoring Program to Improve the Spelling Test Performance of Low-Income, Third- and Forth-Grade Students." *Education and Treatment of Children,* Vol. 10, No. 2, May, 1987.

Marino, Jacqueline L. "Children's Use of Phonetic, Graphemic, and Morphophonemic Cues in a Spelling Task." Ed.D. Thesis, State University of New York at Albany, 1978.

McSweeney, Miriam J. "Word Usage Techniques in Spelling." Ed.D. Thesis, Boston University, 1959.

Morris, Darrell. "Meeting the Needs of Poor Spellers in the Elementary School: A Developmental Prospective." *Illinois School Journal,* Vol. 66, No. 2, 1987.

Petty, Walter T. "An Analysis of Certain Phonetic Elements in a Selected List of Persistently Difficult Spelling Words." Ph.D. Thesis, University of Iowa, 1955.

Read, Charles. *Children's Categorization of Speech Sounds in English Research,* Report No. 17. Urbana, IL: National Council of Teachers of English, 1975.

Read, Charles. *Children's Creative Spelling.* London: Routledge & Kegan Paul, 1986.

Read, Charles, and Richard Hodges. "Spelling." *Encyclopedia of Educational Research,* 5th ed. New York: Macmillan, 1982.

Rinsland, Harry. *A Basic Vocabulary of Elementary School Children.* New York: Macmillan, 1945.

Schroeder, Howard H. "An Analysis of the Use of Visual and Auditory Perception in Spelling Instruction." Ph.D. Thesis, University of Iowa, 1968.

Simmons, Janice Louise. "The Relationship Between an Instructional Level in Spelling and the Instructional Level in Reading Among Elementary School Children." Ed.D. Thesis, University of Northern Colorado, 1978.

Sitton, Rebecca A. "Spelling Instruction: A Dilemma for the Resource Specialist." *California Resource Specialist Journal,* Vol. 10, No. 5, 1990.

Sitton, Rebecca A. "A Turning Point: Three Critical Connections in the Spelling Curriculum for the Nineties." *The California Reader,* Vol. 23, No. 4, 1990.

Sitton, Rebecca A. "Achieving Spelling Literacy: A No-Excuses Approach." *The California Reader,* Vol. 30, No. 1, Fall 1996.

Sitton, Rebecca A. "What Works in Spelling." *Learning Magazine,* September 1995.

Sowers, Susan. "Six Questions Teachers Ask About Invented Spellings." *Understanding Writing: Ways of Observing, Learning & Thinking.* Eds. Thomas Newkirk and Nancie Atwell. Portsmouth, NH: Heinemann, 1986. 47–56.

Stetson, Elton, and Cheryl Laurent, eds. *Training Teachers to Use Research-Based Strategies Improves Student Achievement in Spelling.* Region V Education Service Center, 1984.

Stetson, Elton, Wendy Taylor, and Frances J. Boutin. *Eighty Years of Theory and Practice in Spelling: Those Who Wrote the Programs Forgot to Read the Literature.* Clearwater, FL: National Reading Conference, 1982.

Templeton, Shane. "Synthesis of Research on the Learning and Teaching of Spelling." *Educational Leadership,* Vol. 43, March, 1986.

Thomas, Ves. *Teaching Spelling.* Agincourt, Ontario: Gage Educational Publishing Limited, 1979.

Thompson, Murry Daniel, Jr. "The Effects of Spelling Pattern Training on the Spelling Behavior of Primary Elementary Students: An Evaluative Study." Ph.D. Thesis, University of Pittsburgh, 1977.

Thorndike, Edward L., and Irving Lorge. *The Teacher's Word Book of 30,000 Words.* New York: Columbia University, 1944.

Tireman, L. S. "The Value of Marking Hard Spots in Spelling." Master's Thesis, University of Iowa, 1927.

Zutell, Jerry. "Spelling Strategies of Primary School Children and Their Relationship to Piaget's Concept of Decentration." *Research in the Teaching of English,* Vol. 13, February, 1979.

Introduction to the Blackline Masters

The ***Spelling Sourcebook 1*** Blackline Masters may be duplicated for classroom use.

1. Preview Master (pages 100, 101)

This master provides a special sheet on which students can record the words for their previews (see Article 4, page 21). The master can be used in single-sheet form for each preview, or several copies could be compiled into a booklet for each student.

There are two forms for this master. Teachers can use the one that best meets their needs. Because the number of Core Words previewed may vary from 2–5 words, one of the two masters should accommodate all grade levels, including any review words.

2. Independent Word Study Blackline Master (pages 102, 103)

This master provides a special sheet on which students can practice their words (see Article 6, page 27 and Article 11, page 49). Students need to be taught how to use the master, but once they are comfortable with the study steps, they can use it independently.

There are two forms for this master. Teachers can use the one that best meets their needs.

3. Words to Learn Master (pages 104, 105)

This master can be used as a form for students to record words to learn. These words can be words missed on a Review (Cloze and/or Dictation Activity) that are being recycled for study at school or at home. Students can study the words using the Independent Word-Study Procedure (see Article 6, page 27), or they can be paired for partner study. Parent and child can work cooperatively in preparation for these tests at home.

Other words appropriate for this blackline master are words for a student's Individualized List (see Article 11, page 49).

The master can be used in single-sheet form, or several copies could be compiled into a booklet for each student.

There are two forms for this master. Teachers can use the one that best meets their needs.

4. Letter Grid Master (pages 106, 107)

This master can be used for the Letter Grid Games (see Reference 4, page 86). There are two forms for this master. Teachers can use the one that best meets their needs.

5. Record Keeper Master (pages 108, 109, 110)

For those teachers who wish to keep an ongoing record of students' spelling performance of the Priority Words in everyday writing, this master furnishes a record-keeping system (see Article 10, page 45)

There are three different forms for this master. Each one is labeled with the word frequencies included in its alphabetical listing. Teachers can use the master that most nearly accommodates the Priority Word frequencies for their students.

Dear Parents,

One way your child is tested for spelling growth is with Cloze and Dictation Activities. In a Cloze Activity, the students are read a story while they fill in story word blanks on their copy of the story. In a Dictation Activity, the students are dictated sentences that they write.

Important words are tested again and again over time in these activities. This careful recycling of words ensures that your child develops long-term mastery of these words. Long-term word mastery for spelling is our goal. Short-term learning in which students study a given list of words for a Friday Test is not our goal. We want your child to learn words for a lifetime.

A Words to Learn list will be sent home to you to show you which words your child missed on these tests. These words have not yet moved into your child's long-term memory. To help your child learn them, discuss and study the words with your child. This will help develop the long-term learning we are working toward.

Please think of these tests as a way that you, your child, and I can get helpful information to aid teaching and learning. Learning to spell is important, it will take place over time through practice, and with this system your child will be learning to spell words—not just for a Friday Test, but forever.

Preview

Form 1

Name

Date

Write	Rewrite
1.	
2.	
3.	
4.	

Form 2

Preview

Name ______________________ Date ____________

Write	Rewrite
1. ____________	____________
2. ____________	____________
3. ____________	____________
4. ____________	____________
5. ____________	____________
6. ____________	____________
7. ____________	____________
8. ____________	____________

Word Study

Form 1

Name

Date

Read ⇨ Spell ⇨ Cover ⇨ Print ⇨ Proofread

1.

2.

3.

4.

5.

6.

Form 2

Word Study

Name ______________________________ Date ______________

Read ⇨	Spell ⇨	Cover ⇨	Print ⇨	Proofread

1. ______________ ______________ ______________
2. ______________ ______________ ______________
3. ______________ ______________ ______________
4. ______________ ______________ ______________
5. ______________ ______________ ______________
6. ______________ ______________ ______________
7. ______________ ______________ ______________
8. ______________ ______________ ______________
9. ______________ ______________ ______________
10. ______________ ______________ ______________
11. ______________ ______________ ______________
12. ______________ ______________ ______________
13. ______________ ______________ ______________
14. ______________ ______________ ______________
15. ______________ ______________ ______________

Form 1

Words to Learn

Name

Date

Form 2

Words to Learn

Name ______________________________ Date ____________

Letter Grid

Form 1

Name

Date

Form 2

Letter Grid

Name ______________________________ Date ______________

Record Keeper
word frequency 1-50

Form 1

Name ______________________________

1 the	18 his	35 when
2 of	19 they	36 we
3 and	20 at	37 there
4 a	21 be	38 can
5 to	22 this	39 an
6 in	23 from	40 your
7 is	24 I	41 which
8 you	25 have	42 their
9 that	26 or	43 said
10 it	27 by	44 if
11 he	28 one	45 do
12 for	29 had	46 will
13 was	30 not	47 each
14 on	31 but	48 about
15 are	32 what	49 how
16 as	33 all	50 up
17 with	34 were	

Form 2

Record Keeper
word frequency 1-100

Name ______________________________

1 the	26 or	51 out	76 its
2 of	27 by	52 them	77 who
3 and	28 one	53 then	78 now
4 a	29 had	54 she	79 people
5 to	30 not	55 many	80 my
6 in	31 but	56 some	81 made
7 is	32 what	57 so	82 over
8 you	33 all	58 these	83 did
9 that	34 were	59 would	84 down
10 it	35 when	60 other	85 only
11 he	36 we	61 into	86 way
12 for	37 there	62 has	87 find
13 was	38 can	63 more	88 use
14 on	39 an	64 her	89 may
15 are	40 your	65 two	90 water
16 as	41 which	66 like	91 long
17 with	42 their	67 him	92 little
18 his	43 said	68 see	93 very
19 they	44 if	69 time	94 after
20 at	45 do	70 could	95 words
21 be	46 will	71 no	96 called
22 this	47 each	72 make	97 just
23 from	48 about	73 than	98 where
24 I	49 how	74 first	99 most
25 have	50 up	75 been	100 know

Record Keeper

Form 3

word frequency 101-200

Name ______________________________

101 get	126 must	151 every	176 below
102 through	127 because	152 found	177 saw
103 back	128 does	153 still	178 something
104 much	129 part	154 between	179 thought
105 go	130 even	155 name	180 both
106 good	131 place	156 should	181 few
107 new	132 well	157 home	182 those
108 write	133 such	158 big	183 always
109 our	134 here	159 give	184 show
110 me	135 take	160 air	185 large
111 man	136 why	161 line	186 often
112 too	137 help	162 set	187 together
113 any	138 put	163 own	188 asked
114 day	139 different	164 under	189 house
115 same	140 away	165 read	190 don't
116 right	141 again	166 last	191 world
117 look	142 off	167 never	192 going
118 think	143 went	168 us	193 want
119 also	144 old	169 left	194 school
120 around	145 number	170 end	195 important
121 another	146 great	171 along	196 until
122 came	147 tell	172 while	197 form
123 come	148 men	173 might	198 food
124 work	149 say	174 next	199 keep
125 three	150 small	175 sound	200 children

Materials Description

Rebecca Sitton's SPELLING SOURCEBOOK™ Series
published by **Egger Publishing, Inc.**
P.O. Box 12248, Scottsdale, AZ 85267
888-WE-SPELL (888-937-7355) • FAX 480-951-2276
Find us on the web at **www.sittonspelling.com**
Contact Rebecca at 480-473-7277
e-mail: **rsitton@sittonspelling.com**

Teacher Resource Books

SPELLING SOURCEBOOK™ 1
NECESSARY FOR TEACHERS OF ALL GRADES
Your source for the "how-to" and "why" for developing, inservicing, teaching day-to-day, and assessing your own language-integrated, skill-based spelling curriculum founded on the best practices supported by current spelling research. Reference resources include 1200 high-use writing words, game activities, and blackline masters.

SPELLING SOURCEBOOK™ 2 (Words 1–400)
NECESSARY FOR TEACHERS OF GRADES 1–4
Your source for skill-based activity ideas to extend every high-use Core Word 1–400. Teachers choose the activities that best meet their students' needs and abilities.

SPELLING SOURCEBOOK™ 3 (Words 401–800)
NECESSARY FOR TEACHERS OF GRADES 5–6
Your source for skill-based activity ideas to extend every high-use Core Word 401–800. Teachers choose the activities that best meet their students' needs and abilities.

SPELLING SOURCEBOOK™ 4 (Words 801–1200)
NECESSARY FOR TEACHERS OF GRADES 7–8
Your source for skill-based activity ideas to extend every high-use Core Word 801–1200. Teachers choose the activities that best meet their students' needs and abilities.

SPELLING SOURCEBOOK™ REVIEWS (Words 1–400)
NECESSARY FOR TEACHERS OF GRADES 1–4
Correlated to SOURCEBOOK™ 2, this is your source for Blackline Master Cloze Activities and Dictation Sentences for practice and assessment of every set of five sequential high-use Core Words 1–400.

SPELLING SOURCEBOOK™ REVIEWS (Words 401–800)
NECESSARY FOR TEACHERS OF GRADES 5–6
Correlated to SOURCEBOOK™ 3, this is your source for Blackline Master Cloze Activities and Dictation Sentences for practice and assessment of every set of five sequential high-use Core Words 401–800.

SPELLING SOURCEBOOK™ REVIEWS (Words 801–1200)
NECESSARY FOR TEACHERS OF GRADES 7–8
Correlated to SOURCEBOOK™ 4, this is your source for Blackline Master Cloze Activities and Dictation Sentences for practice and assessment of every set of five sequential high-use Core Words 801–1200.

WORD-WISE SOURCEBOOK™ Level 1
SUGGESTED FOR TEACHERS OF GRADES 1–2
Your source for the best of Dr. Barbara Schmidt's and Dr. Maurice Poe's laugh-aloud rhymes for learning spelling and language skills. Blackline master poems and activities feature Wordy Birdy.

WORD-WISE SOURCEBOOK™ Level 2
SUGGESTED FOR TEACHERS OF GRADES 3–4
Your source for the best of Dr. Barbara Schmidt's and Dr. Maurice Poe's laugh-aloud rhymes for learning spelling and language skills. Blackline master poems and activities feature Willy Wordster.

WORD-WISE SOURCEBOOK™ Level 3
SUGGESTED FOR TEACHERS OF GRADES 5–6
Your source for the best of Dr. Barbara Schmidt's and Dr. Maurice Poe's laugh-aloud rhymes for learning spelling and language skills. Blackline master poems and activities feature Inspector Clue-So.

SEMINAR HANDBOOK *Increasing Student Spelling Achievement*
Your source for follow-along use during and after live training seminars. Contains over 100 pages of reference information.

Teaching Aids

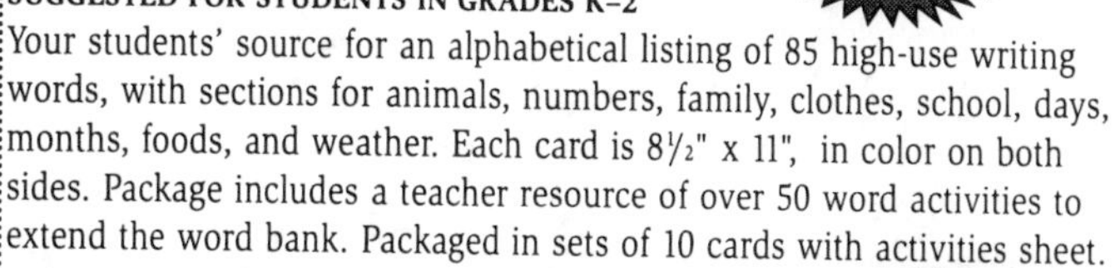

MY SPELL CHECK™ K–2 (pkg. of 10)
SUGGESTED FOR STUDENTS IN GRADES K–2
Your students' source for an alphabetical listing of 85 high-use writing words, with sections for animals, numbers, family, clothes, school, days, months, foods, and weather. Each card is 8½" x 11", in color on both sides. Package includes a teacher resource of over 50 word activities to extend the word bank. Packaged in sets of 10 cards with activities sheet.

SPELL CHECK™ 3–8 (pkg. of 10) NEW!
SUGGESTED FOR STUDENTS IN GRADES 3–8
Your students' source for an alphabetical listing of 150 high-use writing words, with references for months, days of the week, common abbreviations and 75 context sentences for often-confused words. Each card is 8½" x 11", in color on both sides. Package includes a teacher resource of over 50 word activities to extend the high-use word bank. Packaged in sets of 10 cards with activities sheet.

SPELLING WALL CHARTS (set of 5) NEW!
SUGGESTED FOR TEACHERS OF ALL GRADES
Your classroom source for five colorful charts: An alphabetical list of the 100 high-use writing words, context sentences for the *there* homophones, context sentences for the *to* homophones, a prefix poem, and the independent word-study procedure. Each package contains one each of the five different 18" x 24" wall charts.

Training Videos

STAFF DEVELOPMENT VIDEO SERIES
INCLUDES: VIDEO TAPE I — INTRODUCTION TO TEACHERS
VIDEO TAPE II — GRADING AND MANAGEMENT OPTIONS
VIDEO TAPE III — INTRODUCTION TO PARENTS
TRAINING GUIDE FOR STAFF DEVELOPMENT
Recommended for all teachers using the SPELLING SOURCEBOOK™ Series.

Video Tape I (85 min.) An essential introduction to the methodology and recommended follow-up to the training seminar. Rebecca explains exactly how to get started and guides teachers through one complete instructional unit.

Video Tape II (92 min.) Rebecca contrasts Core Words and Priority Words, suggests Priority Word expectations, shows how to grade using six specific options, and provides extensive classroom management ideas.

Video Tape III (37 min.) Assures parental and community support. Rebecca explains why changes in spelling instruction are necessary and how the SOURCEBOOK™ methods ensure spelling success for their children exactly where it counts—in everyday writing. Twelve parent-child spelling partnership activities are suggested.

Training Guide For use with Video Tapes I and II to personalize and extend video training sessions. Includes step-by-step suggestions for the facilitator, discussion-promoting questions, activity-oriented ideas, and blackline masters for making the follow-along handbook for teacher participants.

PLEASE CALL FOR DUPLICATION/BROADCAST CONTRACT INFORMATION.

STAFF DEVELOPMENT SEMINARS
For a fast-paced "how-to" seminar conducted by Rebecca Sitton or one of her associates at your school site, call Egger Publishing, Inc.

FREE Information Package and (on-loan) Preview Video! Call toll free 888-WE-SPELL

Order Form

ORDER ANY 50 BOOKS FOR THE QUANTITY PRICE.

Rebecca Sitton's SPELLING SOURCEBOOK™ Series
published by **Egger Publishing, Inc.**
P.O. Box 12248, Scottsdale, AZ 85267
888-WE-SPELL (888-937-7355) • FAX 480-951-2276

GRADE 1	PRICE	QTY. PRICE	QTY.	TOTAL
Spelling SOURCEBOOK™ 1 . . . . . *The "How & Why" Book*	$ 29.50	$ 24.50	______	______
Spelling SOURCEBOOK™ 2 . . . . . *Activity Ideas for Words 1–400*	$ 29.50	$ 24.50	______	______
Spelling SOURCEBOOK™ Reviews *Assessments for Words 1–400*	$ 39.50	$ 34.50	______	______
GRADE 2				
Spelling SOURCEBOOK™ 1 . . . . . *The "How & Why" Book*	$ 29.50	$ 24.50	______	______
Spelling SOURCEBOOK™ 2 . . . . . *Activity Ideas for Words 1–400*	$ 29.50	$ 24.50	______	______
Spelling SOURCEBOOK™ Reviews *Assessments for Words 1–400*	$ 39.50	$ 34.50	______	______
GRADE 3				
Spelling SOURCEBOOK™ 1 . . . . . *The "How & Why" Book*	$ 29.50	$ 24.50	______	______
Spelling SOURCEBOOK™ 2 . . . . . *Activity Ideas for Words 1–400*	$ 29.50	$ 24.50	______	______
Spelling SOURCEBOOK™ Reviews *Assessments for Words 1–400*	$ 39.50	$ 34.50	______	______
GRADE 4				
Spelling SOURCEBOOK™ 1 . . . . . *The "How & Why" Book*	$ 29.50	$ 24.50	______	______
Spelling SOURCEBOOK™ 2 . . . . . *Activity Ideas for Words 1–400*	$ 29.50	$ 24.50	______	______
Spelling SOURCEBOOK™ Reviews *Assessments for Words 1–400*	$ 39.50	$ 34.50	______	______
GRADE 5				
Spelling SOURCEBOOK™ 1 . . . . . *The "How & Why" Book*	$ 29.50	$ 24.50	______	______
Spelling SOURCEBOOK™ 3 . . . . . *Activity Ideas for Words 401–800*	$ 29.50	$ 24.50	______	______
Spelling SOURCEBOOK™ Reviews *Assessments for Words 401–800*	$ 39.50	$ 34.50	______	______
GRADE 6				
Spelling SOURCEBOOK™ 1 . . . . . *The "How & Why" Book*	$ 29.50	$ 24.50	______	______
Spelling SOURCEBOOK™ 3 . . . . . *Activity Ideas for Words 401–800*	$ 29.50	$ 24.50	______	______
Spelling SOURCEBOOK™ Reviews *Assessments for Words 401–800*	$ 39.50	$ 34.50	______	______
GRADE 7				
Spelling SOURCEBOOK™ 1 . . . . . *The "How & Why" Book*	$ 29.50	$ 24.50	______	______
Spelling SOURCEBOOK™ 4 . . . . . *Activity Ideas for Words 801–1200*	$ 29.50	$ 24.50	______	______
Spelling SOURCEBOOK™ Reviews *Assessments for Words 801–1200*	$ 39.50	$ 34.50	______	______
GRADE 8+				
Spelling SOURCEBOOK™ 1 . . . . . *The "How & Why" Book*	$ 29.50	$ 24.50	______	______
Spelling SOURCEBOOK™ 4 . . . . . *Activity Ideas for Words 801–1200*	$ 29.50	$ 24.50	______	______
Spelling SOURCEBOOK™ Reviews *Assessments for Words 801–1200*	$ 39.50	$ 34.50	______	______

ADDITIONAL BOOKS	PRICE	QTY. PRICE	QTY.	TOTAL
Word-Wise SOURCEBOOK™ Level 1 *Grades 1–2 (Wordy Birdy)*	$ 42.50	$ 37.50	______	______
Word-Wise SOURCEBOOK™ Level 2 *Grades 3–4 (Willy Wordster)*	$ 42.50	$ 37.50	______	______
Word-Wise SOURCEBOOK™ Level 3 *Grades 5–6 (Inspector Clue-So)*	$ 42.50	$ 37.50	______	______
Increasing Student Spelling Achievement *Seminar Handbook*	$ 15.00	$ 10.00	______	______
TEACHING AIDS				
NEW My Spell Check™ K–2 (10-pack) *With teacher resource of over 50 word activity ideas*	$ 5.50		______	______
NEW Spell Check™ 3–8 (10-pack) . . . . *With teacher resource of over 50 word activity ideas*	$ 5.50		______	______
NEW! Spelling Wall Charts (set of 5) . .	$ 8.50		______	______
TRAINING VIDEOS				
Staff Development Video Series. . . *Video Tape I, Introduction to Teachers; Video Tape II, Grading and Management Options; Video Tape III, Introduction to Parents; Training Guide for Staff Development*	$380.00		______	______
Video Tape I	$175.00		______	______
Video Tape II	$175.00		______	______
Video Tape III	$150.00		______	______
Training Guide	$ 30.00		______	______

POSTAGE AND HANDLING

	U.S.	Canada
minimum	$4.00	$8.00
$0–499	8%	14%
$500–999	$40.00	$70.00
$1000 +	4%	7%

No. Items/Subtotal ______ ______
Tax (CA 8.25%, WA 8.2%) ______ ______
Postage/Handling ______ ______
TOTAL ______ ______

BILL TO:

School/District: ______________________
Attention: ______________________
Address: ______________________
City/State/ZIP: ______________________
Phone: ______________ FAX: ______________
Purchase Order No. ______________________
☐ Check ☐ Visa ☐ MasterCard exp. date ______________
Account No.: ______________________
Authorized Signature: ______________________

SHIP TO:

School/Attn.: ______________________
Address: ______________________
City/State/ZIP: ______________________
Phone: ______________ FAX: ______________

ALL PRICES SUBJECT TO CHANGE WITHOUT NOTICE.

WHERE TO SEND YOUR ORDER

TEXAS ONLY
Southwest Schoolbook Depository
1541 Champion Drive • Carrollton, TX 75006
800-266-5122 • FAX 972-241-4390

ALL OTHERS
Northwest Textbook Depository
P.O. Box 5608 • Portland, OR 97228
800-676-6630 • FAX 503-639-2559

Thanks for your order!

Please call Egger Publishing with any questions—888-WE-SPELL (toll free).

Every Child a Speller!